406

A St⚾ry about the Greatest Baseball Game Ever Played

Joseph J. Badowski

ISBN 979-8-89130-133-7 (paperback)
ISBN 979-8-89130-135-1 (hardcover)
ISBN 979-8-89130-136-8 (digital)

Christian Faith Publishing
832 Park Avenue
Meadville, PA 16335
www.christianfaithpublishing.com

Printed in the United States of America

I would like to dedicate this book to my father, Chester A. Badowski Sr. who was able to recover from his alcoholism to become a loving husband to his wife, Florence, a caring father to his four boys, and an awesome grandfather to his many grandchildren.

Prologue

Growing up in a small coal-mining town in Western Pennsylvania, I learned at an early age the importance of hard work, family, and God. My hometown is nestled in the Allegheny Mountains, sixty miles east of Pittsburgh and was the home of around ten thousand people of all diverse cultures and nationalities. My grandfather and grandmother were only sixteen when they came from Poland in 1909 to settle in America. The coal mines were booming back in that time, and Grandfather chose to move himself and his young bride to a place where he could make a good living working in the mines. He came from a farming family in Poland, so his first love was farming. With the money he earned from coal mining, he bought a small farm which he added to each year until he purchased enough land to become one of the largest farms in the area. He and his wife would later have eight boys, all of whom were pressed into service on the farm at an early age. My father, Chester, was the youngest of these boys.

The town's name is Windber, founded in 1897 by the coal baron Charles Berwind, who promptly named the town after himself with a slight modification. It served as corporate regional headquarters for the Berwyn-White Coal Company, and its zenith was the world's leading producer of soft coal. Through their fortunes, the Berwinds systematically built a town of small homes, churches, schools, stores, banks, theaters, and recreational centers. Larger homes and mansions were built on the hills overlooking the town, where executives of the coal mines resided. The smaller houses served as homes for the coal miners' families. My grandfather's farm was located on two hundred acres on the outskirts of town, overlooking the surrounding mountains and valleys.

Life was good for my grandfather and his family living in this small town with a good source of income and some independence that comes from being a farmer. All that came to an end, however, when World War II broke out, and all but one of the boys joined the service. My father forged his birth certificate and, at the young age of seventeen, joined the Navy. Without the help of his sons, my grandfather could no longer maintain the farm, so he sold it and moved into a small home not far away. It was in this home that my memories of my boyhood were formed. After the war, my father returned safely home after serving in the South Pacific campaign. He met my mother, Florence, a nice Polish girl, and got married shortly afterward. I was born in 1953, the oldest of four boys.

Dad worked in the coal mines after getting out of the service and earned enough money to be able to build a small home for his young family. My brothers Mike, Chet, and Tom, along with me were raised from our infancy in this home. We were a strict Catholic family, and my religious beliefs were formed at an early age. I began attending St. John Cantius Polish Catholic School at age six; the first class where first graders did not have to know how to speak Polish to attend school. Before then, English was as second language with all subjects being taught in Polish. I would later regret not having learned to speak Polish from my parents. It was here at St. Johns where I developed my love of God and my Catholic religion, which I would carry with me throughout my life.

Shortly after starting with my schooling, my family was being forced to move from the home he had lovingly built to make room for a highway that was scheduled to be built in the direct path of the home. With reluctance, my dad and mom bought an acre of ground next to a farm on the outskirts of Windber, where they built another home, bigger than the first. This would turn out to be one of the best moves my parents ever made. The home was built on a mountain slope, overlooking the town, and provided us with more privacy. We would all become very proud of this new home. It was here where my mother became pregnant with my youngest brother, Tom.

The year was 1960, and it was then when I first discovered another love of my life, baseball. During the fall of that year, it would later become the fall that I would always remember.

Chapter 1

Opening Day

Nine-year-old Daniel Pryzinski ran as fast as he could down Brereton Street toward Immaculate Heart of Mary Church. He was already late, and school would be starting in a few minutes. It was a sunny but cool April morning. He had stopped at Zinkowski's Grocery Store to buy a pack of baseball cards and now was running late for school.

It was opening day for the 1960 Pittsburgh Pirates, and it was all he could think of this morning. The Pirates were playing this afternoon at Milwaukee. His plan was to listen to the game on the radio after school was over. The Pirates' ace, Bob Friend, was scheduled to start for the Pirates. Milwaukee was the preseason favorite to win the pennant this year. They had a great lineup with Hank Aaron, Eddie Matthews, Al Spangler, and second baseman Red Schoendienst. Warren Spahn would be the starting pitcher for the Braves. Daniel could think of little else as he made his way to school.

Dan could see the domes of Immaculate Heart Church in the distance and knew he had to run faster. The church was one of the oldest Catholic churches in Pittsburgh and is located in the Polish Hill District of the city. The church was founded in 1897 by Polish immigrants who had migrated to Pittsburgh seeking work in the nearby steel mills. His father was a second-generation Polish and worked in the steel mills as did Daniel's grandfather before him. It was a tough job but made a good living for his father, earning enough

1

to help support his family of three boys. The school was located next to the church and was the same school his father had attended, as did his older brothers.

As he ran up the steps toward the school, Daniel could see Father Damian standing at the front door as he did every day before school. Father Damian was the most recently appointed pastor of the Immaculate Heart Church. He was young and very charismatic and well-liked by his parishioners.

Daniel liked Father Damian for another reason: he loved baseball. Father had played baseball at Gannon College in Erie and had been invited to try out for the Pirates when he was in college. Father Damien decided to follow God's calling instead and chose the priesthood as his vocation.

"Good morning, Father," Daniel said, out of breath after running up the steps. "It's opening day today, are you excited?"

Father Damien looked at Daniel and smiled. Daniel was always so full of enthusiasm in everything he did. He was a good student who was always willing to learn. "Yes, Daniel, I'm excited, but don't let the other students know. It's going to be a long season, so let's try not to get too excited."

The Pirates would be playing 154 games this season, so Father Damian's advice was something to heed, but this did not deter Daniel's excitement. He would have a difficult time concentrating on his schoolwork.

It was then that the bell rang. Daniel made his way to his fourth-grade classroom. Sister Mary Agnes was already standing in front of the classroom near the chalkboard. Sister Agnes was a very strict teacher, but Daniel liked her. She had a great way of reaching her students and was always willing to help those students who asked for her help and showed a desire to learn.

Just then, Daniel remembered the package of baseball cards that he had just bought. This was his first pack of baseball cards of the year. Daniel looked at Sister Agnes and then reached into his book bag, where he had placed the pack of cards. He knew that he should wait until after school to open the pack, but he was too excited to wait. He knew if he got caught, Sister Agnes would confiscate the cards. His desire to open the pack of cards overwhelmed him. He had to know which players he got in this pack. So Daniel hid the package underneath his history book, and when Sister Agnes looked away, he quietly opened the pack. There were ten cards in each package. As he opened the pack, he could not believe his eyes. There it was in front of him, the first card in deck, his favorite baseball player and his hero. It was the 1960 card of the Pirates' second baseman, Bill Mazeroski.

Chapter 2

Living with Dad

Bob Prince had been announcing Pirates games since 1947. He was a fiery, brash announcer who was an unabashed Pirates fan. When he announced a game, regardless of the score, he was always entertaining. Prince had his own home run call, "You can kiss it goodbye!" A bang-bang play was "as close as the fuzz on a tick's ear," and the Pirates often missed a double play "by a gnat's eyelash." A sharp single through the hard-packed Forbes Field infield was an "alabaster blast." A Pirate player in slump merely needed the help of some "hidden vigorish." And if the Pirates were trailing in the late innings, Prince openly prayed for "a bloop and a blast" to get them back in the game.

Daniel loved to listen to Bob Prince's broadcast of the Pirates games, so when he turned on the radio to listen to the season opener against the Braves, he was happy to hear the familiar voice of the Gunner, as he was known in Pittsburgh.

Daniel had run home as fast as he could from school and made it just in time to hear the opening pitch. There was a lot of excitement during the offseason about the Pirates' hopes for the 1960 season. They finished a close second place finish in 1958 but had a disappointing season in 1959. The Pirates had not won a pennant in thirty-three years and had not won a World Series Championship in thirty-five years. This year's opening day line-up looked strong, however.

4

Daniel loved to keep a scorecard as he listened to the game. Daniel penciled in the date, April 12, 1960, on his scorecard as he began to enter the starting lineup as Bob Prince announced it over the radio. Leading off was speedy left fielder, Bob "Doggie" Skinner; batting second was first basement Dick "Big Stu" Stuart; batting third was third baseman Don "The Tiger" Hoak; batting fourth was shortstop Dick "The Captain" Groat; batting fifth was right fielder Roberto "Arriba" Clemente; batting sixth was center fielder Gino Cimoli; batting seventh was Bill "Maz" Mazeroski; batting eighth was catcher Hal "Smitty" Smith; and batting last was pitcher Bob "The Warrior" Friend.

After completing the Pirates' line-up, he followed with the Braves' line-up. After it was completed, Daniel looked at the completed line-up score card and frowned. "The Braves look good this year," Daniel opined to himself. "This is going to be a good game."

The Braves scored first in the bottom of the first inning. Red Schoendienst walked and went to second, and Eddie Matthews hit a single. Joe Adcock singled to drive in Schoendienst. One–nothing Braves after one. The score remained one–nothing until the bottom of the seventh when the Braves starting pitcher, Warren Spahn, hit a home run over the right field wall. Daniel began to feel very uneasy after this home run. "How could you let a pitcher hit a home run?" Daniel complained to himself. He began to feel frustrated.

Things changed, however, in the top of the eighth when the Pirates scored two runs to tie the game. Hal Smith led off the inning with a single. Bob Skinner drove Smith in with a double to center field. Clemente tied the game with a single which drove in Skinner. Daniel's spirits lifted. Bob Friend was out of the game, however. Now it was up to Elroy Face to keep the Braves from scoring.

Elroy Face was nicknamed "The Baron of the Bullpen." He was also known as "The Little Man" because of his diminutive size, five-eight, 155 pounds. He had been signed as a free agent by the Pirates on December 1, 1952. He had quickly become one of the best relievers in baseball. In 1959, Elroy went 18 and 1 as a relief pitcher, which was a major league record for a relief pitcher. Daniel felt more than confident the "The Barron" would keep the Braves scoreless for the rest of the game.

Henry Aaron led off the bottom of the eighth with a single. Then the Pirates nemesis for the game, Joe Adcock, hit a home run to make the score 4 to 2. Daniel's heart sank deep as he heard Bob Prince describe the Adcock home run. Face was able to get the next three batters out, so the Pirates had one last time to try the score in their half of the ninth inning.

Daniel screamed as leadoff hitter Gino Cimoli hit a double to right field. To Daniel's despair, his hero, Bill Mazeroski, was pulled from the line-up for pinch hitter Smoky Burgess. Daniel became even more frustrated when Burgess grounded out. He quickly forgot his frustrations when Hal Smith hit a double to drive in Cimoli to make it a one run game with only one out.

Daniel was now standing up, rocking back and forth with anticipation and excitement. Rocky Nelson was the next batter. As he listened to Prince's play-by-play, Daniel's excitement turned to frustration when Nelson grounded out. Now they were down to their last chance. Leadoff hitter Bob Skinner was the next batter. Daniel sat, saying a prayer, requesting God's help to let Skinner get a hit that would tie the game. It was not meant to be as Skinner ended the game with a ground out.

Daniel was drained. It was not a good way to begin the season. The Pirates had outhit the Braves 11 to 9 but could not get the hits when they needed them. *Oh well,* Daniel thought, *it is only the first game of the season.*

He remembered Father Damian's advice earlier in the day: "It's going to be a long season, so let's try not to get too excited."

Daniel had been listening to the game in his bedroom and was paying little attention to anything else. As he turned off the radio, he could hear the commotion going on downstairs. He walked over to the bedroom door and opened it a crack. He could hear his mother crying as his father was yelling at her. He had come home from work drunk again. It had become almost a daily event. His father would stop at a local bar on the way home from work, and when he got home, he would normally start a fight with someone in the family, usually his mother.

Daniel closed the door and lay back down on his bed, sick to his stomach of the thoughts of having to go downstairs to face his father. As he lay there on his bed and began to cry, nothing was important to him now, not even baseball. He wondered why God punished his family so and why he couldn't make his father stop drinking.

Chapter 3

Pittsburgh Steel

Andrew Carnegie was a Scottish immigrant who founded the US Steel Corporation in 1901. Through his hard work and ingenuity, Carnegie was able to build his steel empire into the country's first billion-dollar corporation. With this prosperity came opportunities, and the Polish immigrants were among many nationalities who took advantage of it in order to make a better living for themselves and their families. The US Steel Corporation was built on guts and hard work of these immigrant workers. The Pryzinski family settled in Pittsburgh's Polish Hill in 1919, following the path that Andrew Carnegie had made for them along the Allegheny, Monongahela, and Ohio rivers of steel that formed the boundaries of the City of Pittsburgh Pennsylvania.

Peter Pryzinski was the oldest of three boys born to Frank and Caroline Pryzinski shortly after the Polish couple had moved to Pittsburgh from Poland. At age twelve, Peter was already over six feet tall. By the time he enrolled in Pittsburgh's North Catholic Hill School in 1939, he was six-foot-five, clearly the largest boy in the entire school. Despite his size, Peter elected not to play football in high school to the disappointment of the North Catholic athletic department.

Soon after World War II broke out in 1941, Peter dropped out of school in his junior year to join the Navy. Although he was only seventeen, Peter forged his birth certificate, which managed to get him enlisted. He got his basic training in Chicago along Lake Michigan and was then sent to the South Pacific where he served on an LSD (dock landing ship). These were smaller ships designed to support amphibious landing of men and equipment onto hostile shores. They were heavily protected in a convoy of larger battleships as their firepower and means of self-protection was minimal. During the war, Peter saw his share of casualties. The horrors of war would come back to haunt Peter later on in life.

After the war, Peter returned to Pittsburgh, looking to get his life back on track. The steel mills were booming, and Peter's father convinced him to get a job working at the US Steel plant. He took an immediate liking to making steel, and his union took an immediate liking to Peter. His size made him an imposing figure among his coworkers, and his good work ethic pleased his shift foremen. He was a smart man with good leadership and communication skills. These attributes made him a good candidate for shop steward, a position which Peter would achieve within two years of joining the union.

Things were good for Peter. He was working at a job where he was making good money, and it was a good time for him to settle down, get married, and start a family. In 1947, he met and fell in love with Pauline Piatek, a beautiful young Polish girl whose family also lived in Polish Hill. They married shortly afterward and had three boys. The youngest, Daniel Pryzinski, was born in 1952.

Whether it was the pressure of supporting a young family or pressures from the added responsibilities as shop steward or a delayed reaction to postwar anxiety, Peter began to start drinking heavily. This sudden change in his personality and temperament had a devastating effect on his wife. Up to this point in their marriage, Peter had been a kind, loving husband and father. She couldn't have asked more from a man. She searched for some explanation but had difficulty in understanding why her husband was suddenly drinking so much. As time went on, the drinking became worse to the point that Peter was coming home drunk almost every day.

In 1959, the Steelworkers Union went on strike. The strike lasted 116 days and ended with little benefit to the union members. As shop steward Peter was actively involved in communicating with the union membership, providing daily status reports and updates as to the progress of the collective bargaining. Peter did not support the union's decision to strike. He knew that competition from foreign steel producers like Japan and Korea would be strong and poise future threats to domestic steel producers like US Steel.

Surprisingly, Peter remained sober during the entire length of the strike. Afterward, however, he went on a weeklong binge during which time Pauline never saw her husband. It had been a bad year for the Steelworkers Union and the Pryzinski family, so when the clock turned midnight, marking a new year and new decade, Pauline prayed that things would get better for her husband and her young family.

In 1960, Pittsburgh had just experienced fifteen years of redevelopment that reestablished it as not only a powerful industrial city but also as a dynamic city. The New Year brought with it great expectations and hopes for a bright future. There was also a bright man war hero who was running on the Democrat ticket for President of the United States. He was also the first Catholic candidate since Al Smith, so the Polish Catholic blue-collar workers of Polish Hill were excited with the possibility of having a Catholic President.

As spring approached, the talk turned to baseball in Pittsburgh. Peter wasn't much of a baseball fan. He had always preferred to follow football and always regretted not playing football when he was in high school. He was a Pitt Panther and Pittsburgh Steeler fan. Neither team had much success over the past several years. The Panthers had won eight national championships from 1900 to 1937 but then started to deemphasize the sport. The Steelers had drafted St. Justin's High School product Johnny Unitas in 1955 in the ninth round of the draft but cut him before the season had started. The Steelers head coach felt that Unitas was not smart enough to play quarterback in the NFL.

In 1957, the Steelers traded away their top draft pick for veteran players. The Cleveland Browns used the Steelers pick to draft Syracuse's standout, Jim Brown. So Peter's interest in baseball began to pique as 1960 Pirate team was one of the preseason favorites to win the pennant. His son, Daniel, loved baseball and loved the Pirates. He had always promised to take Dan to see a game, maybe this year.

Peter worked the first shift and was getting near the end of his shift. He started working at the mill as a stove tender, operating the hot blast stoves for two blast furnaces. It was a tough, dirty job, so he went to school where he learned to become a welder. Welders are considered skilled labor, paying an higher hourly wage than most steelworker jobs. It was still hard work, so Peter enjoyed stopping off at the local Polish Falcons social club after work for a few beers. Today, however, he had promised his wife to go food shopping for Easter Sunday, which fell on April 17 this year. He didn't want to be late. He was going to make perogies and kielbasa, his favorites. His parents and two brothers would be joining them for Easter dinner.

As he walked to his car, he heard a familiar voice. "Hey, Pete, wanna grab a beer? The Pirates are playing an afternoon game. It's the first game of the season." It was his buddy, Derek Johnson. He and Derek had started at the mill together and have been friends ever since.

"Sorry, D, but I need to get home today," Peter replied.

"Come on, Pete, just one beer. You'll be home in plenty of time." They both usually met at the Polish Falcons Club in Polish Hill, not far from his house.

Peter did not need too much encouragement; after all, what's one beer? "Okay, I'll meet you at the bar."

This is how it always started for Peter. It's as though he never realized how much he drank. That afternoon, he met Derek, but he had more than one beer. He wasn't interested in the game. He felt comfort sitting at the bar on the same barstool, surrounded by people he knew. It was his escape from reality. The alcohol gave him strength and comfort. He lost track of time, sitting there, consuming one beer after another. Someone from the Pirates hit a double, and everyone in the bar went crazy. Peter didn't care. He hated baseball; he asked the bartender for another beer. He didn't know why his son liked baseball; it was boring.

"Give me a shot of Polish Moonshine," Pete said. That was his nickname for PM Whiskey, which he always managed to drink to go with his beer. The crowd standing at the bar was watching the TV when the Pirates game ended. They had lost, and the crowd began to leave the bar.

"Gotta go big, buddy," said Derek. "See ya tomorrow." Peter felt alone as he got up from the bar stool. He stumbled forward and fell against Derek. "You okay, Peter? You'd better sober up before you get home. Pauline's gonna kill you!"

Peter felt angry. Why should his wife be mad at him? *She knows I work hard. I deserve a few drinks to unwind after work.* His feeling of angry grew stronger as he got out of his car and walked to the front door of his home. As he opened the front door, Pauline was standing there and greeted him. "Peter, you're drunk. Where have you been?"

That was all Peter could handle, and he began screaming at his wife. Pauline looked at him and started to cry. It was starting all over again.

Chapter 4

Eureka Stores

"Slow down, Adam. You're going to run someone over." Nine-year-old Adam Brodziak turned around to see his father walking behind him. It was Friday evening, and they were at the Eureka Department store. They were there to see his mother, who worked every Friday night on the second floor men's department. This was their normal Friday routine, but today was different. They were actually going to buy something. Easter Sunday was only one week away, and Adam was there to get a brand-new suit. He hated to try on clothes. He never felt comfortable trying them on.

"Hurry up, Dad," Adam replied. "I want to see Mom." His mom usually bought him candy when he came to visit her at work. That was part of the fun of his Friday evening visits. His mom wouldn't let him eat candy during Lent. His dad walked with a noticeable limp from a broken leg he had suffered when he was a young man working in the coal mines. His dad was a miner who had started working for the Berwyn-White Coal Company while he was still in high school. The broken leg had kept him out of the service during World War II, something Adam felt that his father always regretted. He had stayed at home instead and kept working in the mines.

Adam loved to ride the escalator to the second floor of the department store. Christmas was always a fun time at the Eureka. Santa was always on the second floor where kids could visit him to give him their Christmas list. His mom played Santa's elf one year.

Adam wished it was Christmas as he jumped onto the escalator. He liked Easter, but it wasn't the same. He didn't believe in the Easter Bunny. He looked behind him and saw his father getting onto the escalator and smiled. He loved his dad. Adam was the oldest of three boys and, as such, enjoyed a special bond with his father. Although he never told Adam, he sensed that he was his father's favorite.

He jumped off the escalator as it carried him to the second floor and quickly made a sharp right turn and ran toward the men's department. He didn't want to wait for his dad. "Hi, Mom" Adam said as he ran to his mother and hugged her.

"Adam, sweetheart, where is your father?"

"He's right behind me, Mom."

Kathryn Brodziak was a young-looking woman with natural blonde hair and a cute dimple in her chin. She had been working at the Eureka since high school. Although she really wanted to study to be a nurse, she did not want to leave home to go to school. She had met his father, Ben Brodziak, while she working in the candy department of the store. Her sister, Anna, was very smart and had left to attend Columbia Medical School when his mom was only a kid. Anna never returned home after becoming a doctor, and his mom seldom heard from her. Kathryn loved her home and family and didn't want to give up the life she loved. Together with her husband, they were able to provide a comfortable lifestyle for their young family. Just then, Adam's father finally caught up. His mother beamed and smiled as she kissed her handsome husband. "Hi, honey. Have you two had dinner?"

"Yes, dear," replied his father. "I made some fishcakes and perogies for the kids before I came over." His mom was a great cook and always made enough perogies to feed her family before she would go to work.

"Excuse me, miss. Can you help me?" asked a customer.

She had to get back to work. She winked at Adam and bent down and gave him a kiss. "Run along now," she told Adam. "I need you to try on some suits for Easter."

Adam smiled but wasn't happy at the prospects of trying on clothes.

"Okay, Adam. We need to go to the boys' department to get you a suit and hat." His dad always made him and his brothers wear hats to church. They hated wearing hats and resisted wearing them whenever they could. His brothers were lucky. They got to stay home with Aunt Patty this evening and didn't have to endure this torture.

"Big Ben, how are you doing?" It was Stan Watroba, the manager of the boys' department. His dad didn't really care too much for Mr. Watroba but always treated him kindly.

"I'm doing fine, Stan. Here to buy my son a new suit. Kathy told me you have some on sale today."

"Sure do," replied Mr. Watroba. "We just received a new shipment today. Let's see what size we'll need to fit this big guy."

Adam hated this but knew better than to complain. Adam looked around the store as he was being measured. The Eureka was the main company store back in the days when the coal barons ran the town and dictated that the miners had to do all of their shopping at the store, which was owned and operated by the coal company. They charged high prices for the goods they sold there, which forced many miners to use store credit to pay for what they purchased. This form of economy made many miners forever indebted to the company store. Luckily, those days were long gone. The store was now owned and operated by a number of local businessmen, who had just purchased the store from the Berwyn-White Coal Company who were planning to close their mining operations.

"So, Ben, how do you think the Pirates are going to do this year?" His dad was an avid baseball fan and followed the team very closely.

"They didn't get off to a good start this week," his dad replied. "That's never a good sign."

Adam was not much of a sports fan. His dad always wanted him to watch the game with him whenever the Pirates were on TV. He never showed much interest.

Adam preferred to read. During summer break from school, Adam would sit in the apple tree in the family orchard and spend all day reading. This past summer, he had discovered a book written by Walter Farley entitled *The Black Stallion*. The book was about a young boy by the name of Alec Ramsey and his beloved beautiful black stallion, which he named "The Black." Adam wanted to grow up and become a vet and maybe raise horses. His dad didn't understand his love of horses but never said anything to discourage his son's interest in them. Adam was sure that he would have preferred his son to grow up to be a professional baseball player.

Mr. Watroba had finished his measurements and had pulled out a suit that he thought would fit. "How do you like this suit, young man?"

Adam didn't care one way or another and just nodded. After trying on the suit, Stan and his dad stood there, looking at Adam. The suit was itchy, and Adam wanted desperately to take it off. "We'll take it," his dad replied.

Adam sighed in relief and wondered if his mom would also like it. Dad didn't usually make these types of decisions. Adam had a sneaking suspicion that he'd be back trying on suits once his mother got sight of this suit. As if he were reading his mind, his father told Stan, "Better have the wife look at this before we buy it. Take the suit off Adam so that I can show it to Mom."

He sighed again as he made his way back to the dressing room. This is why he hated to try on clothes. Why couldn't his mom just pick one out for him without trying it on?

"Wait here, Adam," his dad said as he returned from the dressing room.

Where is he going? Adam thought as he handed over the suit to his dad. *I hope he doesn't take long.*

Soon afterward, his dad returned. "She doesn't like this one, Stan," he said sheepishly. "She'll come down on her break to pick one out. At least we know the size."

Adam was relieved knowing that he didn't have to try on any more suits. Thinking they were through, Adam was ready to go over to the candy department when his dad insisted on Adam trying on a new hat. Why couldn't his mom pick out a hat as well? Obediently, Adam tried on one hat after another until, finally, his dad found one that he liked. It made him look ridiculous, thought Adam, but all he wanted to do was to get out of the boys' department. He was beginning to understand why his dad didn't like Mr. Watroba. "Do you want to show it to Kathy?"

His dad looked across the store and could see that the men's department had gotten busy. He didn't want to bother his wife again. "No, we'll take it."

Adam smiled in thanksgiving. "Let's get out of here already," Adam said to himself.

Adam and his dad walked back to the men's department, carrying their new purchase. "Look what we bought," Ben said as he opened the bag.

His wife was busy but took enough time for her son and husband. She looked in the bag and said nothing. Adam was sure that she didn't like the hat, but she looked up and said, "He'll look handsome wearing that to church."

Okay, they both like it, so let's get some candy.

His father smiled. "What time will you be home?" he said to his wife.

"Probably around nine thirty. We're real busy."

"Okay, dear, we'll see you then."

As they walked through the revolving doors of the department store, Adam's father grabbed his hand. "Let's go home, son," Ben said. His hands were big, rough, and calloused. They were the hands of a coal miner, one who had worked many years in the coal mines surrounding their little town Windber, Pennsylvania.

Chapter 5

King Coal

The Allegheny Mountain range of Western Pennsylvania rose from the southwest part of the state, northeast toward the southern border of New York. They are technically part of the Appalachian Mountains which stretch from North Carolina up through New England. The Alleghenies were the first frontier of the Americas, initially habituated by the Iroquois and Lenape Indians. It was here in these mountains that young George Washington, then a colonel in the British Army, first made his name fighting under General Edward Braddock against the French and Native American Indians. In 1794, after becoming the first president of the United States, President George Washington would send an army back into these mountains to quell a group of farmers who were protesting against the tax that had been placed upon the whiskey they were producing. This act against the "Whiskey Rebellion," as it came to be known, established the government's right to enforce laws and taxes by use of force when necessary.

The mountains run parallel to one another and are connected by wide valleys and vistas, which provide spectacular views from all directions. Contained within these mountains is a vast number of natural resources, the most abundant of which is coal. It was the country's ever-growing need for coal that encouraged the Berwyn-White Coal Company in 1897 to purchase a thirty-thousand-acre farm from David J. Shaffer. This farm was located high up in the mountain range of Allegheny, known as the Chestnut Ridge. Beneath this land was vast deposits of coal, enough to provide a coal supply for not only the country but also for the entire world. The coal company quickly began to place their plan into action: to build a town that would serve as a regional headquarters for their operations, and more importantly, provide housing for the miners they would need to mine the coal.

The design of the town was not typical to other mining towns of the era. The idea was to design a town with wide streets, with a main tree-lined avenue that would provide corporate headquarters, a theater, and a business district. Small single homes were then built around this main street. These homes were unlike most coal mining houses that were normally built as twin or rowhouse type constructions. These homes would provide spacious living for the mining families that would occupy them.

From the main town area, homes were built northward as fingers leading from the town to the entrance of Mines 35 and 40, as they were called. These were the two main mines of the Berwyn-Coal Company, from which millions of tons of coal would be mined over the next seventy-five years.

Fifteen miles to the west lay the City of Johnstown, a city that had been devastated by a flood in 1889, killing over 2,200 people, when a dam located fourteen miles above the city burst during a heavy May rainstorm, sending 20 million gallons of water rushing into the city. Johnstown had been the home of the Cambria Ironworks, which had been badly damaged but not destroyed in the flood. The city, along with the ironworks, was recovering, and coal was needed to fuel the blast furnaces of these mills. This demand provided the Berwyn-White Coal Company with a large, local customer with an unlimited demand for coal.

Windber would also need railroad service to facilitate the transportation of the coal once it was mined from the earth. Altoona, Pennsylvania, was located thirty miles northeast of Windber and served as a railroad hub for the region. The coal company was able to connect rail transportation through Altoona to provide link they need with their customer. The Berwyn-White Coal Company was now poised to make a fortune from the mining of coal. All they needed now were laborers to work in the mines.

The town was built quickly, using trees harvested from the surrounding mountains. It was located in a narrow valley known as the Paint Creek Valley and was built north of the banks of the Big Paint Creek. They named the town Windber, a transposition of "Berwind" from the corporation's name, Berwind-White. It served as a model of efficiency for the burgeoning coal industry. The design of the town left plenty of room for expansion, which was sure to come as miners and their families came to work and live. As the town grew, it would serve to provide the surrounding rural areas with a business district, post office, and churches for worship.

The lure of this newly constructed town combined with the prospects of work in the mines began to attract workers to Windber. With the onslaught of immigration of families in the early 1900s, workers from Poland, Slovakia, Russia, Italy, and other Central and Mediterranean countries, Windber's population began to soar. Few of these immigrants knew how to speak English, and the Berwind-White Coal Company immediately began to take advantage of their newly found source of labor. This began an era in American history where coal miners had to fight for the rights and freedoms guaranteed to them under the Constitution of the United States but that were deprived of them by the coal company owners.

The new and spacious homes that the coal company had built were never made available for sale to these miners. Instead, the mining families were forced to rent these homes from the coal company at high rent and with the threat of immediate eviction if the rents were paid late. A department store was built in town and provided food and clothing for the workers but at higher-than-normal prices. Mining families were forced to buy at the company store, which came to be known as the Eureka Store, named from the various veins of coal surrounding the town. Company spies infiltrated the workers to make sure that families were using the Eureka Store to make all of their purchases. These spies also reported on any efforts by the miners to organize their workforce.

Although the Civil War had ended thirty-six years earlier, a new form of slavery had evolved in the mountains of Western Pennsylvania, one that would not end without bloodshed and without an Act of Congress, which did not come until Franklin Roosevelt's New Deal.

In 1906, over five thousand miners, a vast majority being non-English speaking immigrants, gathered in Windber to strike against the unfair economic and work conditions that they were forced to endure. The Berwind-White Coal Company hired Pinkerton guards to provide security. In reality, these guards were there to attempt to break up the gathering and to bust the striking miners. On April 16, 1906, what started as a peaceful march turned into what was later referred to as the "Windber Massacre."

Unprovoked by the miners, the Pinkerton security force began to randomly fire shots into the crowd of marchers, killing four people, including a ten-year-old boy, and seriously wounding seventeen others. The three men killed were all miners, all foreign-born migrants who had come to Windber from Central Europe. The strike of 1906 ended with nothing gained by the miners to end the slave-like conditions in which they worked.

In 1921, the Windber miners struck again. This time the strike would last over two years. To attempt to break the strike, the Berwind-White Coal Company evicted hundreds of miners from their company-owned homes, forcing many to live outdoors in tents, enduring the harsh weather conditions associated with living in these mountains. The coal company was under contract with the City of New York to provide coal that the city needed to build its subway system. When the mayor of New York learned of the harsh conditions that the miners were living under, he formed a commission to investigate firsthand the conditions and to make an effort to peacefully end the strike. His intervention worked but with little gain to the striking workers.

The oppression by the coal barons would continue until Congress passed legislation in the 1930s to provide controls over the coal companies and protection of the rights of coal miners. By that time, however, the mining in Windber had reached its maximum production levels. The Berwind-White Coal Company could no longer force their will onto their workers, without incurring the wrath of the federal government. This was the beginning of the end for coal mining in Windber, Pennsylvania. By 1960, the company was on the eve of closing their operations in Windber, and in 1962, they terminated all operations.

The region in and around Windber formed the heart of America's Industrial Revolution, a time of great wealth and prosperity for America but also a time of unbridled oppression of American workers. The times required tough men and women who had the strength to live and work and raise families despite the conditions and oppression that they had to endure.

Chapter 6

Easter Sunday

Easter Sunday morning was always a bustle of activity at the Brodziak household. Today was no exception. Adam was the first one up, followed closely by his younger brothers, Gregory and Joseph. On the dining room were three Easter baskets, each filled to the brim with candy. Joey was the youngest and still believed in the Easter Bunny.

"Look what the Easter Bunny has brought you boys!" his mother said, full of excitement. Mom was like a kid herself and enjoyed watching her boys have fun during the holidays. She always went out of her way to make sure that each basket had equal amounts of Easter candy so that there would be no fighting. She had not let her children eat candy during the entire Lenten season; now they were ready to make up for lost time.

The boys tore at the basket, filled with colored plastic hay, to get to the sweet treasures within. Adam's favorite was the white chocolate. He was extremely disappointed later on in life when he found out that there was no chocolate in white chocolate. But now he was in his glory; in his basket was a large white chocolate Easter bunny and white chocolate cross. His mother made sure that each basket contained a cross to remind the boys the reason they were celebrating Easter to begin with. For now, all they could think of was the candy, not thinking much of anything else. They knew that they would have to get dressed soon for Mass, the thoughts of which they chose, for the moment, to forget.

"No candy until you eat your breakfast!" his mother warned.

Easter Sunday breakfast at the Brodziak family consisted of traditional Polish food—kielbasa served with hard-boiled eggs, horse radish and beets, and homemade bread. Adam always enjoyed this part of Easter Sunday. The food they were eating had been blessed by Monsignor Slovinsky on Holy Saturday. Families would lay the food on the altar at church for the priest to bless. It was then the custom to eat the blessed food on Easter Sunday morning as a reminder that Lent was over and to give thanks for the food that God had provided. The blessing of the Easter foods is a tradition dear to the hearts of every Polish family. Being deeply religious, they are grateful to God for all his gifts of both nature and grace. As a token of this gratitude, they have the food of their table sanctified with the hope of that spring, the season of the Resurrection.

After breakfast, his mom would allow each child to have one piece of candy before getting dressed for church. Adam was in his bedroom, looking at the new suit that his mom had picked out. He never had a chance to try on this one and wasn't looking forward to putting it on. His brothers got to wear his hand-me-downs. He hated to get dressed for church, but his father insisted that his boys look presentable whenever they went to church, which was every Sunday at the Brodziak household. Today, the church would be crowded, so Adam knew his father would want to leave early to get a seat so that all of his family could sit together.

Surprisingly, the suit his mom had bought was comfortable and not itchy like the one that he had tried on. It actually felt good to wear! Things were looking up. After putting on his shoes, Adam grabbed his tie and ran downstairs. "Mom, can you help me put this thing on?" It was a clip-on tie, nothing fancy, but Adam always had a hard time putting it on. His mother grabbed the tie and, careful not to pinch his neck, gently clipped the tie to his shirt.

He could smell his father's cologne. His dad was in the downstairs bathroom, had just shaved and showered and, as always, applied a generous amount of aftershave. His dad walked out of the bathroom, looking handsome in his suit and tie, his eyes still wearing the coal miner's mascara that was always difficult to remove, no matter how hard one tried. "Are the boys ready, Kate?" his dad said anxiously. "I don't want to get there too late."

"Yes, dear, they're almost ready," she replied. His mother knew how to deal with her father's anxieties, and her mannerisms always had a calming effect on her husband.

"I want to take some pictures of the boys before we leave." He had gotten a new Kodak Brownie Hawkeye camera for Christmas and now thought of himself as an amateur photographer. So, whenever the occasion presented itself, his father would gather everyone to take pictures. It was a bright sunny cloudless morning, perfect for taking pictures on the front lawn of their home.

"Where is your hat, Adam?" his father asked.

He had hoped that his dad had forgotten about the hat, but no such luck. He ran upstairs and retrieved the hat that his mother had laid on his bed. By the time he ran downstairs, the rest of the family had already assembled in the front yard. The grass was still wet from the early morning dew, but that didn't deter his father. His mother, on the other hand, looked dismayed as the boys' brand-new Easter Sunday shoes were getting wet. She didn't say a word, however, and obediently arranged her sons in order of size for their picture.

Adam turned to look at the house behind him as his mother was fooling with his two brothers. He loved their home. His dad and Uncle Ed had built this house together, and the family had moved in only a few years ago, when Adam was still in kindergarten. It was located on a hill next to Berkley's dairy farm, overlooking the valley and town below. His dad never graduated from high school but somehow had acquired the knowledge to build this house from the ground up. The property was located away from town, and the adjacent farm gave extra privacy for their family. There was an orchard on the property as well, with apple, cherry, and plum trees. One of the apple trees grew large green apples that, when ripe, tasted like bananas to Adam. He always referred to the fruit that grew on the tree as banana apples. At the top of the orchard stood the large McIntosh apple tree, where he would climb each summer and read his books. The tree provided an even greater view of the town and surrounding mountains, and he would get lost for hours, sitting in that tree, reading.

"Turn around, Adam," his father demanded. He looked to see his two brothers standing next to them. They looked miserable, and Adam suspected he looked the same way. All three were standing there in their Easter suits, wearing their goofy hats, their feet getting wet standing on the grass. Greg was the second oldest, born a year and a half after Adam. Joey was the youngest, who was only five. "Now smile, boys," his father pleaded. They looked like gangsters standing there with their hats and suits. No one smiled as his father pressed the button on his Brownie to snap the picture.

"Okay, everyone, into the car. We're going to be late." His dad owned a two-toned, blue-and-white Ford Falcon, which was barely big enough to fit everyone. He also owned an internal truck that his grandfather had given to his dad when he first got married. He used the truck for work, and it was always dirty with coal dust. The family packed into the Ford Falcon, and they were off to church.

Although the address was Somerset Avenue, the road leading from the Brodziak home was more of a private road, a quarter of a mile long, which ended at a tree where you had to turn left to get to the main road. The main street of Windber was called Graham Avenue and ran about five miles from Rummel to the east, through the town to Scalp Level in the west. The main street was tree-lined. with homes and businesses lining each side of the road. They had to turn right onto Graham Avenue in order to get to church.

They passed Windber High School, which was built of Graham Avenue just before you got to the main downtown business district of Windber. It was the home of the Windber Ramblers High School football team, which was the pride of the town. The school had been founded in the early 1900s and, ever since, had become legendary for its great football teams. The schools was nicknamed the Ramblers because the team was willing to go anywhere in Pennsylvania to play football. They would normally do so, playing teams from much larger cities as Johnstown, Altoona, Harrisburg, Erie, and Pittsburgh. The Ramblers had won two state championships over the years, one in 1933 and the second in 1936. This was no small accomplishment since at its heyday, the population of Windber was never more than ten thousand.

Frank Kush was a Rambler standout and had played on the 1954 Michigan State National Championship team. Rumors had it the Frank was getting ready to move to Arizona to become head football coach at Arizona State. Adam's dad loved Frank because he was Polish and belonged to the parish and was the son of a coal miner.

As they passed the school, Adam could see the twin spiral steeples of St. John Cantius Church. It was the largest building in Windber and could be seen from miles. It was a beautiful church, designed like those churches found in Poland. They stopped for a red light at the intersection of Fifteenth and Graham. On the corner was Windber fire station, and across the street was the Arcadia Movie Theatre. His Aunt Patty would take him and his brothers there to see a movie almost every Saturday, provided that there was something good to see. Adam wanted to see the new Walt Disney movie *The Absent-Minded Professor*; he would ask Aunt Patty to take him to see it when it came to the Arcadia. Up Fifteenth Street to his right, Adam could see the Eureka Store, where his mom worked. The light turned green, and his father drove forward.

St. John Cantius Catholic Church was built in 1909 by Polish immigrants. Next to the church was the school that taught first through eighth grades. Adam was in the fourth grade. The classrooms were small and accommodated two grades in each room. His brother Greg was in the second grade. Joey was attending kindergarten at a public school. He would start next year at St. John Cantius.

Adam's Uncle Frank, his father's brother, was the custodian of the church and school, and he greeted them as his dad pulled into the parking lot of the church. "Did you save us a seat, Frank?" Ben asked as he shook his brother's hand. The boys jumped from the car and hugged their uncle.

"Happy Easter, Uncle Frank!" they cried in unison. "Are you coming to our house this afternoon?"

His mother always had Easter dinner at their home, and this year was no exception. Uncle Frank lived with his grandma and grandpa, and Mom always invited them over on Easter. "I sure am," Frank replied. "Did the Easter Bunny treat you guys okay this year?"

Before they could reply, his father pushed them along, anxious to get inside and find a seat. "See you this afternoon, Frank. Come hungry."

Frank nodded as he watched the Brodziak family hurry into church.

His parents were devout Catholics and raised their family accordingly. Their kids were taught at an early age the importance of their Catholic faith and how that faith combined with love of family was the cornerstone of everyday living. It was their belief that love of God and love of family were the most important things in life; if one trusted and believed in both, all else would be provided and hardships overcome. His father blessed himself with holy water, and the rest of the family followed behind.

They were fifteen minutes early for Mass, but the church was already packed with people. His dad was quick to find a pew to seat the entire family. They had been instructed by their mom to remove their hats when they entered the church. Now they clipped them onto tiny hangers located on the back of the pew in front of them. The entire family knelt in prayer, then rose as Monsignor Slovinsky entered the sanctuary as bells announced the beginning of Easter Sunday Mass.

Monsignor Slovinsky had been Pastor of St. John's for the past thirty-five years. He spoke fluent Polish, which was a necessity when managing a parish consisting of many Polish-speaking parishioners. He had been named Pastor shortly after the miners' strike of 1922. He knew what the importance Catholic faith had in the lives of hard-working miners whose families made up most of his congregation. For these reasons, the Polish workers were dedicated to their church and to Monsignor Slovinsky. They always donated their time, labor, and treasure willingly to support their church. His sermons were also given in both English and Polish, which made most Masses run longer than normal.

Although both of his parents spoke and read Polish, they never taught their children, something Adam would regret later on in life.

Easter Sunday would be no different from the pulpit as Adam had to endure a lengthy bilingual sermon. Adam thought Mass would never end. He was looking forward to getting back home to enjoy the Easter candy that was waiting for him there.

The choir began to sing Polish songs as Monsignor Slovinsky gave his final blessing, marking the end of Mass. As he left the pew, Adam genuflected, a sign of reverence to God, and proceeded to follow his mom and dad from the church. Soon he would be home and out of his suit. "Grab a church bulletin, Adam" his father said as they were leaving church. "I need to speak with Uncle Frank before we go home. I'll meet you at the car."

It was around two in the afternoon when his grandpa, grandma, and Uncle Frank had arrived at their home. His mother had already been cooking for two hours and was ready to serve her Easter Sunday dinner. His grandparents spoke little English, so it was always hard for Adam to talk with them. They had married when they were only seventeen and had come to America in 1916. Grandpa came to Windber and began working in the mines. With the money he had earned working in the mines, he bought a small farm on the outskirts of town. Each year, he would buy more land around the farm until eventually he owned one of the largest farms in the region. Eight boys were born to his grandparents, the youngest being Adam's father.

When World War II broke out, all but Adam's father was able to serve. His Uncle Joe had been killed at D-Day, but the rest had returned safely home following the war. Four years of war took its toll on his grandfather, however, and without the help of his boys, he was forced to sell the farm. Now they lived in a small twin home with his Uncle Frank on the outskirts of town.

His dad was reading the church bulletin when they arrived. He greeted them with the customary Polish greeting, "*Jak się masz.*"

"Did you see this, Frank?" his father said, pointing to the bulletin. "The church is sponsoring a bus trip this summer to Pittsburgh to a Polish festival and to see a Pirates game. We gotta go and take the kids with us. What do you think?"

Adam's uncle loved baseball but wasn't too keen on traveling to Pittsburgh on a bus full of kids. Pittsburgh was sixty miles west of

Windber, and it took almost two hours to get there. His uncle just smiled. Sensing his reluctance, Ben Brodziak coaxed him, "We can get to see Bill Mazeroski play in person."

"We'll see," replied his uncle. "We have plenty of time to decide."

The Pirates were playing an Easter Sunday doubleheader today, which made his dad wonder who would leave their families to see a baseball game, let alone two games.

Adam grabbed the bulletin after his father and uncle left the room. He didn't follow the team but knew that Bill Mazeroski was his dad's favorite Pirate. Adam supposed he liked him because he was Polish. He read the brief announcement.

> Come join us the weekend of July 16th and 17th to a Polish festival at the Immaculate Heart of Mary Polish Church in Pittsburgh. The cost includes bus fare, and tickets to Sunday's Pittsburgh Pirates doubleheader baseball game vs. the Cincinnati Reds. Members of the Immaculate Heart of Mary Church, have volunteered their homes so that we can stay overnight, free of charge.

The furthest he had been away from home was a visit last Christmas to nearby Johnstown. His mother had taken him there on a bus to do some Christmas shopping. Traveling to Pittsburgh for an overnight stay sounded like a great adventure; seeing a baseball game, however, didn't seem much like a fun idea.

Chapter 7

Polish Festival

"Bingo, I have Bingo!" shouted someone from across the crowded Bingo Hall. The basement of the Immaculate Heart of Mary Church served as a Bingo Hall every Tuesday evening from seven until ten. The hall held 220 people comfortably and was used to host many social events of the parish, including weddings, church socials, as well as Bingo. As was normal for every Tuesday Bingo night, the hall was filled to capacity.

"Check the card, Marty," instructed George Zanecky. The Knights of Columbus ran the Bingo night for the parish, and George was the Grand Knight for the Immaculate Heart of Mary Counsel. George normally served as the caller for Bingo and Marty Adams one of many of the Knights of Columbus who assisted.

The anticipated winner held her hand up as Marty made his way to her table to check her card. This had to be done after every Bingo call in order to confirm a winning call. Mary Lewitze was waiting for Marty as he approached her table. "Good evening, Mary. Do you have a winner?"

Mary said nothing in response. She played Bingo every Tuesday and took the game very seriously and was in no mood for conversation. She had played twelve Bingo cards, which was normal for her. They were spread out in front of her. At the top was a little porcelain doll that she brought and placed at her table for good luck.

"These Bingo players are nuts," Marty said to himself as he began reading the numbers, loud enough for George to hear. "B-10, I-19, N-30, G-43, O-60," Marty recited, waiting for George to confirm each number. "We have a winner!" George confirmed. After a short break, they would begin the next round.

Pauline Pryzinski worked in the kitchen and behind the counter with five other women from the parish every Tuesday. She brought her three sons with her to help as well. She wanted them to be involved in the parish and felt having them help at Bingo would be good for them. They would go from table to table, taking orders from players and delivering food and coffee. On occasion, the boys would receive nice tips. The boys had fun and competed with one another to see who could get the most tips. Whether it was because he was the youngest or the cutest or whether it was because he worked harder than the other two, Daniel always seemed to get more tips. This always made the older boys mad. She encouraged the boys to save their money and had opened a saving account for each of them at the local bank.

Her oldest son, Michael, was in eighth grade at Immaculate Heart and would be graduating this spring. Luke was her middle child and was in the sixth grade. Michael was somewhat of a bully at school, and he tormented the two younger children, especially Daniel. Michael was tall and handsome, like his Father, and planned on playing football at North Catholic in the fall. He was, no doubt, his father's favorites son, something that Peter did not conceal from the others to her dismay.

Although she did not want to admit it, Pauline always favored Daniel. He was a hardworking, intelligent young man, who Pauline knew would grow up to be successful. Luke was the quiet one, who struggled with schoolwork, and was always off to himself. Pauline worried about him the most because she realized that he was most like her. Pauline was always a shy person, who struggled to talk with others that she did not know. She saw in Luke the same personality and knew that he, too, would have problems growing up.

Shyness was not a good quality, especially for a young man growing up in a blue-collar community. She knew that he would have a tough time opening up to people and showing his emotions. Although she was close to her boys, she was never one to say too much to them, especially when it came to the affairs of the family.

"Hello Pauline. How are you doing this evening? It looks like we have another full house this evening." George Zanecky was taking a break and, as was his custom, made a point to say hello to Pauline. He and Pauline had dated in high school, but she broke off with him. George had just been elected Grand Knight of the Knights of Columbus Council, a position that suited him well. Unlike most men from the parish, George did not work in the steel mills. After graduating from high school, George attended the University of Pittsburgh and then went to Duquesne Law School.

To his credit, he stayed in Polish Hill, where he opened his law practice. Although he was more of a general practitioner, George did a lot of work for the steelworkers of the community, helping whenever he could to provide legal advice and to assist whenever a worker was injured on the job. His reputation spread throughout the steelworker's union members, and he began representing clients from throughout the city. He was well respected in the community and in the parish, where he was always first to volunteer. Surprisingly, George had never married.

Pauline enjoyed talking to George, and he always made her feel comfortable. "How's Peter doing?" George asked. "I haven't seen him around in a long time. Is everything okay?"

Peter had joined the Knights of Columbus shortly after they were married and had actually served one year as Grand Knight. He no longer got involved with the Knights or with any Parish activities and, in reality, seldom went to Church anymore. "He's been working the late shift," she lied. "I hardly get to see him myself." She wondered if George really knew the problems she was having with her husband.

"Well, tell him that I said hello and that we miss him. I've got to get back to calling Bingo. Looks like our customers are getting restless."

She wished that he had stayed longer to talk as she watched him return to the podium. Pauline looked around the hall as George began to call his numbers. She had met her husband at a social the parish had for returning veterans from the war. Her husband was tall and distinguished, wearing his Navy uniform. She fell in love with him the moment they met. They danced, and he told her jokes the entire evening. When the social was over, he walked her home and kissed her good night. A year later, they were married. They were married in a beautiful service in the church, and then had their reception in this this hall. It was the happiest day of her life. She prayed every day that God would return the man she loved so much back to her.

Around ten o'clock, Father Damian made his appearance, a sign the Bingo for the night was to end shortly. Father was a very charismatic man, and although he was much younger than the two other priests assigned to the parish, he commanded a great deal of respect among the parishioners. Pauline was behind the counter as he approached. "Good evening, Pauline," Father greeted, "how did we do tonight?"

Pauline was preparing to close the register but could tell from the brisk business that they had taken in a lot of money from the sale of food and beverages. Before she could answer, Father Damian asked, "Pauline, I need to ask a favor of you."

Pauline looked at him in wonder. He had never asked her for a favor in the past and was surprised that he even knew who she was.

"I would like for you to become a member of our Polish Festival committee this year. We need all the help we can get." Father Damian's plan was to send invitations to all of the parishes in the three-county area, inviting them to come to the festival. He planned to end the weeklong festival by offering tickets to a Sunday afternoon Pirates game. Although it was only April, plans had to be made well in advance to reserve tickets with the Pirates' front office.

Pauline hesitated. This was a lot to ask of her. Surely her husband would not be too happy with the idea; however, it was hard to say no to this priest. Despite her apprehensions, she felt a sense of belonging and need, which she had never felt before. "Okay, Father," she reluctantly responded. "Just let me know what you want me to do."

As he walked away, Pauline wondered what she had gotten herself into. She also needed to find a way of breaking this news to her husband.

Chapter 8

The Plan

"Hey, squirt, do you want to go to the Pirates game on Sunday?"

Daniel looked up from the book he was reading to see his brother Mike standing over him. Now his brother Mike hardly ever said two words to him, and when he did, it was either to borrow money or to make fun of him or to beat him up for no reason but for his own personal enjoyment. So Daniel was skeptical as he asked, "You have tickets?"

"No," replied to Michael, "we're going to sneak into the game. Jay Dinger got in through the bleacher side gate last Tuesday when the Pirates played the Cubs. He wants us to go on Sunday to see the Giants play."

Daniel knew that it was too good to be true. Jay Dinger was his brother's best friend, who was always getting into trouble. He was suspended for a week from school last month after getting caught smoking in the boys' room at school. "Mom and Dad will kill us if we get caught!" Daniel replied.

"Don't be a sissy. You gotta take a chance every once in a while. Besides, I know how much you love the Pirates. Come on, little brother, I'll watch out for you."

That was the thing Daniel feared the most: relying on Michael to do anything responsible was always a problem. But the prospect of seeing the Giants play the Pirates was too appealing to pass up. The Giants had Willie Mays and Willie McCovey on their team. I would be great to see them play in person. Home games were never tele-vised, so the alternative would be to sit in his bedroom all afternoon and listen to the game on his radio. "Okay," Daniel agreed, "but what are we going to tell Mom and Dad?"

"I have that figured out," Michael responded. "I'm telling them that Jay's dad got us tickets and that we're going with him to the game. We'll meet at Jay's house, then catch the bus to Forbes Field."

Daniel began to feel more comfortable with this plan, providing that they did not get caught getting in. "Okay Mike," Daniel replied, "count me in."

*****

Sunday morning, May 22, 1960, was bright and sunny as Daniel woke and started to get ready for Mass. He was serving as altar boy for the ten-thirty Mass. This was his first year serving as altar boy, so he didn't want to be late. The thoughts of going to the Pirates game that afternoon proved to be a major distraction. He could hardly contain his excitement. He still didn't know how they were going to get into the game without tickets, but that was of no concern to him at this point. He was leaving that part of this adven-ture up to his older brother. As he was daydreaming about the game, his brother walked into his bedroom. "We're leaving right after you get home from Mass." His brother had served the seven-thirty Mass and was ready to leave. "I told Mom that we Mr. Dinger had tickets and we're going with him, so we're all set to go."

Their father had come home drunk again last night, and the two had fought late into the night, so he suspected that his mother had other things on her mind this Sunday morning and wasn't in the frame of mind to question her oldest son.

"Daniel Pryzinski," he heard his mother call from downstairs, "are you ready for Mass yet? I don't want to be late."

Daniel gathered the black cassock and white vestments his mother had ironed the night before and ran down the stairs to greet her. "I'm ready to go, Mom," he said with enthusiasm. He looked at her face and could tell that she had been crying. He knew better than to say anything to her. More and more these days, his mother was always crying. Although she never spoke to her sons about her feelings and what she was dealing with, the boys knew that their parents were not getting along very well. For some reason, however, his mother kept everything to herself, trying to hide the fact that her husband was a drunk.

Daniel felt sorry for his mother and was embarrassed by his father, but there wasn't much an eight-year-old boy could do about it. He knew his mother was trying desperately to keep the outside world from knowing that her husband had a drinking problem. A thing like that is hard to keep quiet in the tight-knit Polish Hill community. His friends never said a word to him, but they were too young to understand anyway.

Michael was the closest to his father, and Daniel knew that he was taking his father's drinking troubles very hard. Whenever Daniel tried to talk to him about his father, Michael would get very angry with him. "Dad doesn't have a problem he can't deal with," Michael would say in defending his father. Daniel could tell that Michael was feeling really bad but had learned not to talk about the issue. Since he received no consolation from either his mother or his older brother, Daniel decided, when the time was right, to talk to Father Damien.

The ten-thirty Mass was High Mass, which meant that Mass would normally be longer than usual, requiring most of the parts of the Mass to be sung and the use of incense. So by the time Daniel got home, it was nearly noon. The game began at 1:05 p.m., so he knew that his brother would be anxious to get going. "I thought you guys would never get home," Michael said as he and his mother entered the door. "Come on, Danny, we got to get moving!"

His mother kissed both goodbye and told them to have a good time. "Hope the Pirates win!" she said as they walked out the door.

"Let's run. We're meeting Jay at Bigelow Boulevard," Michael said as he started to run.

Daniel ran as fast as he could but had a hard time keeping up, so by the time he got there, Jay and his brother were already waiting. "Hurry up, Dan," Jay said as he saw him across the street. Jay "Ding Dong" Dinger, as the kids called him at school, was a good foot smaller than Mike. Daniel never liked the kid and often wondered how his brother got to be so friendly with him. Ding Dong was always getting into trouble at school and, unlike his brother, had no athletic skills at all. He tried to join the CYO baseball team in the spring but was so bad that he had to be cut from the team.

"Okay, boys," he said as Daniel joined the duo, "this is what we're going to do. I painted these pennies silver last night, and we're going to use them to ride the bus to the game." Daniel looked at the pennies and rubbed them. The paint was coming off in his hand. This was never going to work. "Here are the tickets to the game."

Daniel looked at Jay in disbelief. "I thought we didn't have tickets!" Daniel looked at the ticket Jay gave him. *What is this?* Daniel said to himself.

"After Tuesday's game, I hung around and picked up a bunch of torn ticket stubs. I then pasted them together. They look legit, don't they?"

"No!" replied Daniel, constraining his emotions not to scream at Ding Dong. "This is never going to work. We'll get caught sure as we're standing here!"

His brother slapped him across the head. "Shut up, Daniel," Michael said. "Got a better idea?"

At this point, Daniel just wanted to go home but said nothing. He should have known better than to trust these two knuckleheads.

"Here comes the bus, get ready."

Jay was the first one in and, without hesitation, placed the pennies into the toll catcher and walked into the bus. His brother followed and got on the bus. As Daniel was trying to throw his phony dimes into the catcher, he dropped one onto the floor of the bus. The driver looked at him and patiently said, "Take your time, son. Is this your first time on a bus?"

Daniel had ridden the bus many times with his mom, but this was the first time that he was trying to cheat on the fare. Daniel picked up the silver penny and made his deposit. The driver looked away, closed the bus door, and drove on. Daniel made his way to the back of the bus to join Jay and his brother. *This may work after all*, Daniel thought. Nevertheless, he was feeling guilty and had an uneasy feeling that this adventure was not going to work out. Jay and Mike were talking, ignoring him. The bus moved forward. It was only a fifteen-minute bus ride to Forbes Field, and his excitement began to rise at the thoughts of seeing the Pirates play.

Chapter 9

Forbes Field

The bus ride to Schenley Park and Forbes Field took fifteen minutes, during which time Jay and Michael schemed their plan to get into the game. The tickets that Jay had patched together really did look authentic if you weren't looking at them too closely. Although he was still feeling guilty about the whole thing, Daniel began to feel hopeful that this was going to work. He also imagined that they would get caught and all hell would have to be paid with his mom and dad.

The bus came to a screening stop as the driver yelled, "Forbes Field!"

The boys jumped up, not realizing that they had made their destination, ran to the front of the bus, then jumped off behind a fat lady that was wearing a Pirates cap and carrying a "Beat 'em Bucs" pennant. Daniel looked up at the street sign. "Forbes and Bouquet," he read. His grandfather had taken him to a game when he was four, but he hadn't been to see a game since. He could hardly remember what it was like.

The bus moved on, leaving the trio on the sidewalk. A trolley car was pulling up on either side of the streets, so the boys maneuvered their way across the tracks to the other side of Forbes Avenue. Daniel had no idea in what direction to go. There was a restaurant on the corner. Daniel read the sign: Frankie Gustine's Bar and Restaurant.

He committed that name to memory as a landmark for their return, wondering who Frankie Gustine was.

There were hundreds of people walking in one direction, which Daniel assumed was the direction to Forbes Field. "Do you guys know where to go?" Daniel asked, still uncomfortable that his older brother had no clue where to go.

"Just follow the crowds, I guess," said Michael, who also seemed a bit confused as well.

"Follow me!" yelled Jay. "This way!" They continued on Bouquet and walked a block where they made a left onto a street called Sennott. As they turned the corner, Daniel caught his first glimpse of Forbes Field. It looked magnificent to him.

Forbes Field was the second oldest baseball park in baseball. It was built in 1909 by the owner of the Pirates, Barney Dreyfuss. He had decided to build the park away from downtown Pittsburgh in the Schenley Park District, near to the University of Pittsburgh. With help from his friend, Andrew Carnegie, he was able to build the park at a cost of a million US dollars.

Unlike other baseball parks of that era that were made from wood, Forbes Field was built in three tiers, using steel made in Pittsburgh and concrete. He hired Charles Wellford Leavitt Jr. to design the stadium's grandstand, but it was Dreyfuss and then Pirates Manager, Fred Clarke, who laid out and designed the playing field. They designed a huge playing field with the intent to limit home runs. The distance to the outfield fence in left, center, and right field were 360 feet, 462 feet, and 376 feet. The outfield walls were also built high to limit home runs. Although it was considered to be the ultimate pitcher-friendly field, there had never been a no-hitter pitched at Forbes Field.

Construction began on January 1, 1909, and took only six months to complete, with the first game played on June 30, 1909. The stadium had been named in honor of General John Forbes who captured Fort Duquesne from the French in 1758 and rebuilt and renamed it Fort Pitt.

Daniel now stood at the front entrance gate and looked up in awe. The front of the building turned in either direction at a forty-five-degree angle and raised three stories high. The excitement of getting onto the park to see the game was overwhelming. "This way," Jay directed as they walked through the crowd to the left field bleacher side of the stadium. It was decided on the bus ride over that they would gain entrance through the bleacher side of the park. The tickets were cheaper in that section of the park, and more importantly, the seating was unnumbered, so you could sit anywhere, and no one could bother you, providing that they were able to get in.

Jay and Michael ran ahead, and it was difficult for Daniel to keep up. The large crowds also made it difficult to see his brother. He was now afraid of getting lost in these crowds. Despite everything, however, Daniel was able to follow and finally met up with the boys as they stood in line at the bleacher side entrance. "Can you guys wait for me?" Daniel complained. "I don't want to get lost!" His complaints met deaf ears as he was ignored by Jay and his brother.

"Okay, guys, here are the tickets. You're going to have to hold your thumb over the tear in the ticket that I passed together. When we get to the gate, show the ticket to the attendant but try not to let go of the ticket. Let the guy just tear off the stud."

Daniel looked down at the ticket. It was the first time he saw it this close up and was impressed how perfectly the stubs had been glued together. *Leave it up to Ding Dong to come up with this idea.*

The crowd was pressing tighter as the boys made their way toward the entrance gate. Daniel began to feel anxious, and his heart raced. Jay was the first one to reach the gate. Daniel looked at him as he held the ticket. The attendant barely looked at him as he tore the stub from Jay's hand. He was in! His brother was next and had no problems. As Daniel approached the gate, he could see his brother and Jay on the other side, inside the park, slapping one another on the back. He only hoped that they did not take off without him before he got in. The attendant looked down at Daniel as he held out his ticket. "Who you with, kid?" he said.

Daniel froze, and he struggled with what to say. Surely, he was going to get caught. "I'm with my brother," Daniel finally said, pointing in the direction of where Michael and Jay were standing.

Without saying another word, the attendant tore the ticket from his hand and looked away.

He made it! *This goofy idea actually worked!* Daniel thought as the anxiety he was feeling was replaced by joy and excitement.

"Told you this would work," Jay said with a prideful smile. "You guys should know better than to doubt good old Jay Dinger!"

Daniel looked around in amazement. He could hardly believe that he was in Forbes Field and that he was actually going to see the Pirates and the Giants play in person on this beautiful Sunday afternoon. For Daniel, this was better than Christmas.

Chapter 10

Love of the Game

The boys hurried their way underneath the concourse, following the signs above leading them to the bleacher section of Forbes field. As they were walking, Daniel could smell the aroma of hot dogs, popcorn, and peanuts. Suddenly, he felt hungry. He hadn't eaten since breakfast, and the smell of food roused his appetite. In his haste to meet up with Jay Dinger at the bus stop, Daniel had forgotten to bring money. He always kept some of the money he made from bingo in a tin can, which he hid underneath his bed. It was only used for emergencies and to buy Christmas or birthday presents. Now he wondered how he was going to pay for food and only hoped that his brother had brought money, although knowing his brother, he had little hope that his brother would treat him. Stealing food, if that was the alternative, was out of the question. Daniel was feeling guilty enough and would starve first before entertaining that idea.

As they walked up a ramp from the concourse to the bleacher section, Daniel was blinded by the bright sunlight. Before him was the emerald green field of Forbes Field, surrounded by a necklace of golden-brown dirt marking the infield and foul lines in each direction, leading from home plate. The ground crew was busy marking the foul lines and the batter's box. They had gotten to the game too late to see batting practice, but there were still plenty of players from both teams on the field, stretching, running, and throwing baseballs to one another. It was a marvelous sight for young Daniel.

The Pirates were wearing their traditional black, gold, and white uniforms. The front of their jerseys bore the team's name, Pirates, and their baseball caps were black, adorned with a golden P in front. Daniel was proud of the Pirates team colors and the uniforms they wore. Ironically, the San Francisco Giants had similar colored uniforms, black and cream with orange lettering with the initials SF blended together in orange color on a black cap. *No one should wear orange*, Daniel thought, *especially a professional baseball player.*

From where they were standing in the bleachers, Daniel had a good view of left and center field. His eyes searched the field until he found him. There he was, standing is center field, the great Willie Mays. As he watched, Willie ran back toward the center field wall. Someone standing outside the infield on the grass had hit a ball, and it sailed deep to center field in the direction of Willie Mays. It looked to Daniel to be long enough to reach the outfield wall and maybe go over it. Daniel could only see his number 24 as Willie turned and galloped from his standing position and, without what appeared to be much effort on his part, reached up and caught the ball right at the base of the wall. *What a great catch*, Daniel thought, silently wishing that Willie Mays was a Pirate.

The Pirates had their own version of Willie Mays. His name was Roberto Clemente. Clemente had been drafted by the Pirates in 1954 by former General Manager Branch Rickey. He was the first Latino player to be drafted by a Major League baseball team. While Rickey was the GM of the Brooklyn Dodgers, he had gained notoriety for drafting the first Negro player by the name of Jackie Robinson. Clemente played right field and was an outstanding all-around player. Like Willie Mays, Clemente was known for his fielding prowess, making circus-like basket catches and throwing out runners with bullet-like throws from his outfield position. When a player got a hit toward him in right field, Clemente was known for running to the ball, fielding it in one hop, and throwing the runner out at first base—a very difficult thing to do. Daniel looked for his familiar number 21 but could not find him anywhere on the field.

Daniel's attention turned toward the infield. He was looking for his favorite Pirate, number 9, Bill Mazeroski. He was considered one of the best second basemen in baseball. The fans all knew him by his nickname, Maz, but Pirate broadcaster, Bob Prince, often referred to him simply as "The Glove." He was known best by the fans for his ability to pivot while turning a double play. Although Maz didn't have a great year at the plate in 1959, he was named to his second All-Star game. He started the 1960 a little thinner, losing weight in the offseason, but as of today's game, he was only batting 211. The fans, however, were here to see Mazeroski play second base. When fielding a ground ball, Maz appeared to be skating around second base, making hard plays appear easy.

Daniel found Maz standing near the Pirates' dugout, signing autographs for a bunch of kids who had gathered for an opportunity to see the second baseman close up and hoping for autographs. Daniel was jealous and wished he were one of those kids. From where they were standing in the bleachers, it would be difficult to walk the distance to where Maz was standing. By the time he got there, Bill would likely be gone. The game was going to start soon anyway.

Just then, Bill turned away from the throng of kids and headed toward the dugout. Even from this distance, Daniel could see the big chaw of tobacco in his cheek, which had become Bill's trademark signature. He played the entire game with that chaw in his mouth, which Daniel thought was promoting an entire new generation of tobacco chewers among his young fans.

Suddenly, all the players exited the field, and Daniel looked up at the huge Longines clock that overlooked the left field, which confirmed that it was one o'clock. It was getting close to game time. While he was obsessing over the pregame warm up, Daniel failed to notice that he was standing there alone. His brother and Jay had taken off without telling him. Daniel shielded his eyes from the afternoon sun, looking behind him, seeking to find his companions among the throng of fans. Rising high in the background outside the park behind the left field bleachers was the University of Pittsburgh's Cathedral of Knowledge. It was an impressive building, one of the tallest buildings in Pittsburgh, and the largest college building in the world. Looking at this gothic building, Daniel forgot about his brother and Jay.

The building formed at perfect union with the nearby land-scape and blended with the spring foliage on the trees in the adjacent Schenley Park. It was a sight that Daniel would remember the rest of his life.

Just then, Daniel felt a slap on his back. It was his brother with Jay standing nearby. "Here you go, squirt," Michael said as he handed Daniel two hot dogs and a bag of peanuts. "You got to be hungry! I am."

Without asking any questions, Daniel grabbed the food, relieved that he finally had something to eat. "Thanks," Daniel responded as he opened and began eating one of the hot dogs. His brother was all right after all.

As he stood there, eating his hot dog, the voice of the public address announcer commanded everyone, "Please stand for the play-ing of our national anthem."

Daniel looked at the flag flying in the spring breeze in the outfield wall. The familiar tune of the "The Star-Spangled Banner" echoed through the caverns of Forbes Field as Daniel crossed his heart in tribute. He looked down at the Pirate players standing in the field with their caps in hand, looking in the direction of the Stars and Stripes. The game was only moments away from starting, but Daniel's attention was fixed only on the playing field, watching his favorite players standing at attention in a field of green surrounded by thousands of fans who stood silently by. They were all paying trib-ute to our nation's flag, but Daniel knew better. The sell-out crowd was there to see their favorite team and was standing to also pay trib-ute to the greatest game in the world: baseball.

Chapter 11

Come-from-Behind Win

The game took three and a half hours to play. It was delayed briefly by a sudden, unexpected spring shower and went eleven innings, but the Pirates won 8 to 7 over the Giants. Daniel sat on the bleachers, looking at the scoreboard, wet, cold, and shivering. He didn't seem to care, though. The Pirates had beaten Willie Mays and the San Francisco Giants, two of three games in this home stand, and were now solidly in first place in the National League.

It had been a great game from the beginning. Vern Law was the starting pitcher for the Pirates, and his mound opponent had been Jack Stafford of the Giants. Both pitchers were their team's respective aces. Jack Stafford broke into the Major Leagues in 1956 with the Philadelphia Phillies and won Rookie of the Year honors in 1957 after finishing the season with a record of 19 and 8. He was traded to the Giants in 1959 and finished that season, going 15 and 12. This was the first meeting of the year for these two pitchers, and everyone was expecting the game to be a pitcher's duel. Instead, neither pitcher got past the fourth inning.

By the top of the fifth, the Giants were winning, 4 to 2. The Pirates tied the game in the bottom of the fifth and then took the lead, 5 to 4, in their half of the sixth when Bill Mazeroski hit a solo home run. It was Maz's seventh home run of the year and came at a crucial time in the game for the Pirates. The Pirates fans and Daniel went nuts as the ball flew over the left field of Forbes Field. Little did Daniel realize at the time, but Mazeroski would hit a home run over the same left field wall to end the 1960 World Series that would forever enshrine Bill Mazeroski into baseball immortality.

The Giants continued to battle the Pirates, and in the top of the seventh inning, they scored three runs to regain the lead over the Pirates. With two outs, Don Blasingame hit a single to left center. Joey Amalfitano hit a double to left field to score Blasingame. The Pirates then intentionally walked Willie Mays with first base open. The next batter was Willie McCovey who made the Pirates pay for walking Mays when he hit a double to left field, scoring Amalfitano and Mays. So as quickly as the Forbes Field fans' excitement rose after the Mazeroski home run, their dejection over the seventh inning rally by the Giants was felt throughout the stadium.

The Pirates went down in order in the bottom of the seventh off of Giants reliever Billy Lowe. Daniel's heart began to fade as Dick Stuart grounded to the Giants' short stop, Eddie Bressoud, to end the inning. There were just two more at bats for the Pirates who were down by three runs.

The Giants continued putting pressure on the Pirates in the top of the eight by drawing a leadoff walk off of Pirates reliever, Fred Green. With one out, pitcher Billy Lowe was safe on an error by first baseman Dick Stuart, while attempting to bunt to advance the runner to second base. Now there were two men on with only one out. To the relief of the Forbes Field faithful, Fred Green was able to work out of the eighth inning jam to keep the Pirates within striking range. The Pirates put two men on in their half of the eighth but were unable to score any runs. After eight full innings, the Giants were still leading, 7 to 5.

Daniel had been watching the bullpen for several innings where he could see the Pirates' mighty mite, Elroy Face, warming up. It was now Elroy's turn to take the mound in relief. Daniel loved to see Face come into a game. He always seemed to have the ability to get batters out, and good things always seemed to happen after Elroy started to pitch. True to form, Face was able to get the Giants out one, two, and three in the top of the ninth. This was now do or die time for the

Pirates. Daniel looked to heaven and said a prayer as the Pirates came to bat. *Could the Bucco's muster a comeback?* Daniel prayed.

The Pirates were now at the top of their lineup, and leading off the ninth was Don Hoak. Hoak was a local boy, born and raised in nearby Roulette, Pennsylvania. He had been a standout all-American basketball player at Duke University before drafted as an amateur free agent by the Brooklyn Dodgers in 1947. To the delight of the Pirates fans, Hoak led off the bottom of the ninth with a walk. Dick Groat was next to bat and hit a soft fly ball to shortstop. So with one out, Pirates left fielder Bob Skinner came to the plate.

At the start of today's game, Skinner was batting a lofty .354 and, along with Clemente, led the team in hitting. His nickname was "Doggie" and was a left-handed batter who threw with his right arm. He had signed with the Pirates right out of high school in 1951 and was brought up to play with the club in 1954. He had already collected two hits earlier in the game: a single and a double. Now the Pirates fans were praying that "Doggie" would come through again and keep the inning going.

Billy Lowe was in his second inning of relief and was ready to pitch to the Pirates slender left fielder. He had to get only two more outs, and the Giants would go home winners. Lowe looked into Skinner and threw the first pitch to him—a fast ball high and inside. Skinner looked at Hoak at first base, waiting for Lowe's next pitch. Skinner looked at the next pitch and took a strike. Lowe began his next delivery, hoping to fool Skinner with a curveball. Instead, Skinner timed his swing perfectly and hit a long fly ball to deep left field. The place erupted as the ball sailed over the ivy-covered wall for a home run. Skinner had done it! The Pirates had tied the game in their last at bat, 7 to 7.

Daniel sat in his seat on the bleacher, his throat hoarse from screaming. Everyone around him was still celebrating as the Pirates rally continued. With two outs, Clemente singled to center field. Smoky Burgess reached base on an error by the Giants second baseman, Don Blasingame, sending Clemente to third base. He couldn't believe it! The Pirate runner was ninety feet away from winning this game. Gino Cimoli was the next batter who hit a harmless fly ball to right field to end the inning. Thanks to Skinner's home run, however, the game was tied, and the Pirates were going into extra innings.

Face stayed in the game in relief for the Pirates and was again able to get the Giants out in order in the top of the tenth. Although the Pirates managed to get two runners on in their half of the tenth, they were unable to score, and the game remained tied going into the eleventh inning.

Now in his third inning of relief, Face would first have to pitch to the Giants' ninth batter before facing the top of their batting order. For some reason, the Giants elected not to pitch hit for relief pitcher Mike McCormick, a decision that they would later regret. McCormick hit an easy fly ball to Mazeroski at second. Face got the next two Giant batters out in order to end the inning. "The Barron of the Bull Pen" had pitched three perfect innings in relief for the Pirates. Now he looked to his teammates to give him the win.

Roberto Clemente was arguably the most exciting player on the 1960 Pittsburgh Pirates team and was probably their best player. The season was still young, and the Pirates' right fielder was already leading the team with a .382 batting average. This was Roberto's sixth season with the Pirates, and his hitting and fielding skills were already widely known throughout both the National and American Leagues. So when he came to bat with one out in the bottom of the eleventh, the fans erupted with chants of, "Arriba, Arriba," a nickname that Pirates broadcaster Bob Prince had bestowed upon Roberto because of his aggressive and dashing style of play.

Clemente promptly responded by hitting a double to right field amidst the screaming of the sellout ballpark. He moved to third on a groundout to second by pitch hitter, backup catcher Bobby Oldis. With two outs, the Giants decided to intentionally walk Gino Cimoli and Bill Mazeroski to get to the Pirates other backup catcher, Hal Smith. So with the bases loaded and two outs in the bottom of the eleventh inning, Smith ended the game with a single to left field, scoring Clemente from third base.

The place went wild as the rest of the Pirates ran onto the field, jumping on Smith and slapping him on the back. Daniel, Jay, and his brother stood with the rest of the crowd, clapping, yelling, and otherwise going crazy jumping up and down on their bleacher seats. The Pirates had done it, coming back to beat the Giants, something that this team would repeat many times during the rest of the 1960 season. Hal Smith and Bill Mazeroski were two of the heroes of this game. The same two would pair up again in the seventh game of the 1960 World Series to become heroes again in a game many feel was the greatest baseball game ever played. This game against the Giants was a turning point for the team and would establish the Pittsburgh Pirates as a strong favorite to win the National League Pennant.

Daniel looked down at the Giants players leaving the playing field, among them number 24, the great Willie Mays. Fortunately for the Pirates, the "Say Hey" kid had gone 0 for 4 in the game but did score a run for the Giants. Daniel followed Mays as he ran from center field until he disappeared into the visitors' clubhouse, still wishing that Mays was a Pittsburgh Pirate.

Chapter 12

Getting Lost

A ray of sunshine broke through the rain-laden clouds hanging above Pittsburgh as the fans began to leave Forbes Field. Daniel turned to see his brother and Jay already walking up the steps of the bleachers, following the rest of the crowd toward the stadium exit. Suddenly, Daniel felt cold, tired, and hungry and remembered the last thing he ate were those two hot dogs he had wolfed down before the game started. He reached into his pocket and felt the bag of peanuts that were still there. It was so late to be fooling with them now. He couldn't wait to get home now. His mom always made a nice Sunday dinner for the family, and she had promised to wait until they got home from the game before starting the meal.

Michael looked back and saw his little brother walking behind him. "Stay close, Danny," he said, "I don't want to lose you now."

Daniel's legs were sore from sitting on the hard bench all afternoon, and he struggled to walk up the steps. He looked at the Cathedral of Learning standing in the background behind the bleachers and again was amazed at his awesome size and architecture as he left the bleacher area along with the rest of the fans. What a great day it had been, he thought, grateful that he had made the decision to accept his brother's invitation. He no longer felt guilty for sneaking in but decided that he would confess this entire day to Father Damien during his next Confession. He hoped that Father Damien would understand.

As they entered the dark tunnel concourse that ran underneath the stadium, Daniel suddenly felt overwhelmed by the number of people that were there trying to get out. When they had first arrived to the game, there were not as many fans trying to get into the stadium. Now the vast crowd was massed together, all trying to leave at the same time. Not too many had left the game early. He panicked as he lost sight of his brother and Jay; they had just been standing in front of him a moment ago. The crowd pressed harder against Daniel as they were being funneled through the small exit passage. They had to be right in front of him, he consoled himself. *Don't panic. Just keep following the crowd.* He felt confident that his brother would be waiting for himself somewhere in the concourse.

The exit signs appeared above his head as he kept looking for his brother. As the crowd slowly filtered through toward the exits, Daniel saw no signs of either Michael or Jay and suddenly felt like crying. He was never a baby and seldom cried but was never alone as he was now in a strange place, with no one to show him the way home. Daniel composed himself as he squirted through the exit way to the outside of Forbes Field. The sun was out full, and Daniel was blinded by the brightness that had been missing for most of the afternoon. He decided to stand outside and just wait for his brother and Jay. There was no sense in walking around and getting lost. At least he was a little familiar with the area where he was standing. This is where the boys had gained entrance to the stadium when the first arrived, which for now, for Daniel, seemed to be a long time ago.

The massive crowd began to dwindle as people turned in each direction to resume leaving Forbes Field to go home. Buses were lined up on the street, waiting to pick up fans that had come far and wide to see the game. Still there was no sign of his brother and Jay. His panic now turned to anger at his brother for being such an incompetent idiot. How could he not have waited for him to make sure he was safe? Daniel had made the mistake again in trusting his brother. Now Daniel had to decide what he was going to do. He remembered the direction the boys had followed from the bus stop to the stadium. He would retrace his steps to the bus stop, where hopefully his brother would be waiting. He panicked again, realizing that he had no money. They had used Jay's silver painted pennies to pay their way on the bus over to the game. Jay never gave him any pennies for the return trip. Daniel decided not to worry about the money now; his goal right now was just to find his brother and Jay.

Daniel followed the sidewalk adjacent to Forbes Field, to where the stadium ended at the intersection of Schenley and Sennott Avenues. He continued across the busy intersection where traffic of cars and buses were congested, trying to get free from the stadium area. He remembered the way now; although he could not remember the name of the street, he did know that they had walked only one block on their way to the game after making a left. So Daniel made a right at the next intersection. He looked up at the street sign which read Bouquet. That street name sounded familiar to Daniel, so he made a right, not 100 percent certain that he was walking in the right direction. Suddenly he saw the sign, Frankie Gustine's Bar and Restaurant, the name he had earlier embedded into his memory as a landmark. Across Forbes Avenue from this restaurant was the place where the boys had gotten off the bus. Daniel again vowed to someday find out who Frankie Gustine was, but for now, his main objective was to find his brother and to catch a bus to get back home. His hope turned to despair as he crossed over the trolley tracks to the other side of Forbes Avenue. Neither his brother nor Jay were anywhere in sight.

A bus pulled up and came to a screeching stop in front of him. Daniel didn't even know which bus they had ridden on to get from his house to the game. He was tempted to get on board and ask the driver for the name of the bus that he would need to take, but before he could do so, the bus door slammed shut, and the bus proceeded on its way. He was uncertain now of his next move as he looked over at Frankie Gustine's Bar and Restaurant. There was a line waiting to get into the place, all Pirate fans there to celebrate the victory, Daniel thought, as his stomach again reminded him that he was hungry. He had remembered when they first arrived at the stadium seeing a sign marked "Pirates Front Office." He decided to truck back to the stadium and ask for help. Maybe Michael and Jay would be waiting for him there. He hoped as he crossed over Forbes Avenue for yet another time.

*****

Jay had yelled to Michael to follow him as they left the bleacher area of Forbes Field. "I know a shortcut to get out of here. We can beat the crowds." Michael looked behind him and saw that his brother was still behind him. Instead of saying something to Daniel, however, Michael followed Jay, assuming that his little brother would follow behind. True to his word, Jay's shortcut turned out to be just that. They had made a right turn after leaving the bleacher area, instead of turning left with the rest of the crowd, and found themselves outside of the ballpark ahead of everyone else. *What a great guy,* Michael thought of Jay as they walked through the exit way.

Michael turned to look for his brother. There was a little kid following him, but it was not his brother. Michael looked at Jay and then simultaneously began to yell, "Danny, Danny!" Michael rushed back toward the stadium but was stopped by a security guard.

"You're not allowed back inside," he warned Michael.

"I lost my little brother. I need to go back in find him," Michael whined.

"Sorry, kid, but I can't let you back inside," replied the security guard, who was obviously taking his job very seriously. "Why don't you go to the front office?" he advised. "Lost kids normally show up there."

Michael grabbed Jay, and they ran as fast as they could toward the front of the stadium, where the front office was located. In their haste, both managed to run right past Daniel, who by this time had exited the stadium. Daniel's back was turned to the two boys as they ran behind him.

"I've lost my little brother," Michael said to the front desk receptionist, out of breath from his run. "I thought he was right behind me!"

"Where are your parents?" was the first the receptionist said in response.

Michael and Jay looked at each other with concern, not willing to reveal that they had no parental supervision. "My dad left the game early to get the car," Jay responded. "We're out of town and parked a mile away!"

The receptionist was a heavyset woman in her late fifties and looked suspiciously at both boys. "What is your brother's name?" she said. "And how old is he?"

Michael looked at Jay in relief. "His name is Daniel, and he is eight years old," Michael replied.

"Does Daniel have a last name?"

"Pryzinski, his last name is Pryzinski, and I am his brother, Michael."

She made Michael spell it then said, "Okay, go find your father and bring him here. I will page the stadium and advise the security guards to keep an eye out for him. Hopefully, we'll find him by the time you get back."

"What do we do now, Jay? My parents are going to kill me if I come home without Danny."

Jay stood there a moment and thought. "We have them looking for Danny here, so why don't we walk back to the bus stop? Maybe he found his way back there and he's waiting for us."

Michael didn't want his parents to know what they had done, so he was afraid that the Pirates front office would call them if they found Danny before he and Jay got back. Against his better judgment, Michael agreed, and the two took off running as fast as they could to get to the bus stop. Little did they know that Daniel had the same idea and at that very moment was walking behind them hoping to meet up at the bus stop.

When they got to the bus station, Daniel was nowhere to be found. They decided to walk a block north toward another bus stop farther up on Forbes Avenue. Maybe Danny had gotten confused and was waiting for them at a different bus stop. When they arrived at this stop, there was no Danny. By this time, Jay was getting antsy. He was already late getting home, and soon he would be in trouble as well. Besides, he never liked Michael's brother. He knew that Danny and his classmates always made fun of him at school, and even though he was older, he had no respect for him. It would serve Danny right to get lost. Maybe it would teach the little bugger a lesson. It was his job to keep up with them, and he didn't. Now Jay had to waste his time looking for him.

"I got an idea," Jay said to Michael as they stood at the bus stop. "It'll take us fifteen minutes to get home on this bus. It would take that long to walk back to the stadium. You can tell your parents that we left the game early and that my dad was with Danny and was driving back with him. I'll call the stadium when I get home to find out if they found him. We could then take the bus back to pick him up."

Even though Michael always agreed with Jay's harebrained schemes, this was more than Michael could take. "That's a dumb idea, Jay!" Michael responded to his friend. Michael did realize that it would be faster to get home. He would tell his parents the truth, accept his fate, and get his parents involved in finding his little brother. Just then, a bus pulled up. "Let's go, Jay. I've got to get home and tell my parents."

Jay looked at him, relieved that he no longer had to be involved in the search. They got onto the bus, paid their phony toll, and sat down and, for the first time all day said nothing to one another. The bus proceeded to the next stop, where it picked up more Pirates fans still celebrating the win. The doors closed without either Michael or Jay seeing little Daniel standing there at the bus stop.

*****

"Your brother and his friend were here about thirty minutes ago," the receptionist told Daniel. "They went to get your father. How far away did he park from the stadium?"

Daniel had walked back from the bus stop and had told the receptionist who he was and that he was lost. Now he looked at her, confused. "I live in Polish Hill and my brother, and his friend and I took the bus here," Daniel confessed. "My father didn't come with us."

The receptionist looked at the security guard who was standing next to her. "I thought those two were up to no good," she said.

The security guard looked down at Daniel. "We need to call your parents, son. Do you know your telephone number?"

Daniel looked at the guard and thought if he looked too young to not know his own telephone number? Instead of saying something smart, Daniel politely gave the security guard his telephone number. He knew that he and his brother were in for it now.

Daniel listened as the receptionist spoke in the phone. After her initial introduction, and explanation for the call, the receptionist turned the phone over to Daniel. It was his mother. She sounded upset and was demanding to know what had happened. Reluctantly, Daniel had to tell her the entire story. There was a strange silence on the other end of the phone as Daniel finished the story. He could tell that his mother was mad. "Okay, young man. Your father and I are leaving right now to come to get you. Do you know where Michael is?"

He had forgotten about his older brother. Now Michael was the one that was lost. "I don't know where he is. I've been trying to find him myself."

His mother was silent again but finally responded, "Okay, just wait there. Hopefully, he'll show up." His mother hung up, and Daniel sighed, knowing full well what was awaiting him when he got home. He handed the phone over to the receptionist.

"My mom and dad are on their way here to pick me up," he advised the receptionist. "Okay," she said sternly. "You can have a seat over there," she said, pointing toward the chairs located in the reception area.

Obediently, Daniel took a seat. He had not taken notice when he first walked in, but there were pictures covering all of the walls of Pittsburgh Pirates players, current and past. Many he recognized and many he did not. Daniel was in his glory, finally realizing that he was in the front office of his favorite team, the Pittsburgh Pirates. Suddenly he heard a commotion coming from the offices located behind the front desk. "Bill, the *Pittsburgh Post-Gazette* would like to thank you for taking this time to meet with us after such a long game. You had a great game today! The Pirate fans are going to love to read all about it in tomorrow's paper!"

A group of men began walking in line toward Daniel, seeking to leave by the same doors that he had entered. At the end of the line, Daniel looked in amazement, and he recognized Bill Mazeroski, wearing a short-sleeved shirt and khaki pants. His distinctive crew cut haircut made him stand out from the rest. The men looked at Daniel as they walked past but said nothing to him. Mazeroski, however, immediately took notice of the little boy and said, "Sally, what do we have here?"

Although he had been there now for quite some time, he just realized that he never learned of the receptionist's name. "This is Daniel Pryzinski, Mr. Mazeroski," Sally replied. "He and his brother snuck into the game today. He got separated from his brother and ended up here. His parents are on their way over to pick him up."

Bill Mazeroski looked at Daniel incredulously and asked, "How old are you, Daniel?"

Daniel looked at his hero, hardly daring to believe that he was standing right in front of him, talking to him. "I'm eight years old, Mr. Mazeroski," Daniel stammered.

"You must be a real Pirates fan to have the guts to sneak into a game. These security guys are pretty tough. You could have gotten arrested," Mazeroski joked.

"I don't care. It was worth it," Daniel said, jumping from his seat. Without thinking, Daniel ran to Mazeroski and hugged him. "You're my favorite player, Mr. Mazeroski. You had a great game. That home run was the best part of the game."

Bill looked at the child and smiled. "Thanks, son," he said. "Fans like you make it all worth the while." He looked at Sally and said, "Do we have any baseballs back there, Sally?"

She immediately left her post and ran to the back where she retrieved a baseball they stored away for players to autograph. "Here you go, Mr. Mazeroski." For the first time since Daniel met her, Sally actually smiled as she handed Bill Mazeroski the baseball along with a pen.

Daniel watched as he scribbled on the ball and handed it to Daniel. He looked at the signature on the ball. "Bill Mazeroski #9" he had written on the ball.

"Gee whiz. Thanks, Mr. Mazeroski," Daniel said in gratitude.

"Next time, you have your parents buy you a ticket and take you to a game. Don't be doing anything crazy like this again."

Daniel had already promised himself that he would never do something as stupid as this again. He looked up at number 9 and replied, "I promise, sir, I'll never try to do this again."

Mazeroski shook the boy's hand and smiled. "Take care, Daniel. Keep on rooting for the Buccos." As he walked through the door, the reporters who were waiting outside surrounded the baseball player again, trying to get the most from him before calling it a day.

Twenty minutes later, his father, mother, and Michael came walking through the door. He glared at Michael without saying a word but was taken by surprise when his father grabbed him and pulled him off the ground. "Are you all right, Danny?" his father questioned as he hugged his son. This was not the response that he had expected from his parents, especially his father. He looked at his father's sober face and marveled. He couldn't remember the last time his father had hugged him. A sense of great joy overcame him as he hugged his father in return. This was better than getting an auto-graphed baseball from Bill Mazeroski. Daniel realized that his father did care for and loved him. Knowing this was better than any Pirate win or any number of autographed baseballs.

*****

Daniel and Michael were grounded for a month afterward. Word about their day at the ball game spread around school, and Daniel quickly became a hero in his fourth-grade class. He hid the ball that Mazeroski had signed in the tin box that he hid under his bed, but he pulled it out every night before saying his prayers and looked at the ball before putting it away in his makeshift safe. Unexpectedly, his brother Michael stopped bullying him and seemed to develop an unexplained respect for his younger brother. Although they didn't talk too much about the entire affair, the boys knew that what they shared that day would be remembered and talked about for the rest of their lives.

As for Jay Dinger, Daniel never spoke to him afterward but realized that if it hadn't been for Jay, the three would have never experienced one of the best times of their lives. The Pirates continued their winning ways, and Daniel hoped that someday he'd be able to return to Forbes Field again before the end of the season. Daniel's wish would come true, greater than he could possibly hope for.

Chapter 13

Immaculate Heart of Mary Church

The Catholic Church has played an important religious, cultural, and political role in Poland ever since AD 966. Ninety-eight percent of people living in Poland identify as being Catholic, so when Polish immigrants came to Pittsburgh, Pennsylvania, most gravitated to the Polish Hill section of Pittsburgh.

To celebrate their Catholic faith, the Polish Catholic residents of Polish Hill helped to build the Immaculate Heart of Mary Church in Pittsburgh, referred to in Polish as Kościół Matki Boskiej in 1904. It is one of the city's oldest and largest churches. (1) The church's three domed, cathedral-style structure overlooks the City of Pittsburgh, serving like a beacon for the surrounding city.

Father Damian Koskyovko had joined the parish in 1955 as an associate pastor and was named the pastor in 1959 at the young age of thirty-nine. His parents immigrated to Pittsburgh after World War I, his father looking for work in the steel mills or the nearby coal mines. While living in Poland, his parents owned a small farm, where they lived off of the land, as was a traditional way of living in Poland. After the war his parents were looking for a better way of life, away from war-torn Europe, and decided to move their family to America.

His parents bought a small home in Polish Hill and began to raise their family. Damian was the youngest of four children, two girls and two brothers. Although they were now American, Damian's father insisted that his children continue to speak the Polish language, when they were alone in their home. He was also deeply religious man and raised his children to become devout Catholics. So when they were of school age, all four children would attend grade school at Immaculate Heart of Mary. His parents' strong religious beliefs, along with his Catholic education, helped Damian formulate his intentions to become a priest early in his life.

Following grade school, Damian attended Central Catholic High School, where he excelled in both academics and sports. He played quarterback for Central Catholic High School football team and, after graduating, received scholarship offers to play football at Pitt, Penn State, and Indiana University of Pennsylvania. Much to his father's dismay, he decided, however, to attend college at Duquesne University, a local catholic college in Pittsburgh. While at Duquesne, he majored in theology and Catholic studies.

Following graduation from Duquesne, Damian entered the seminary at Saint Charles Borromeo Seminary in Wynnewood, Pennsylvania, right outside of Philadelphia, Pennsylvania. After his ordination, his first assignment was to Saint Adalbert Church, located in Port Richmond, Philadelphia. Port Richmond was located in the Polish section of Philadelphia. Because he was fluent in Polish, this parish was a perfect fit for this novice priest.

As luck would have it, following his eight years at Saint Adalbert's, Damian sought and received permission from the office of John Cardinal Dearden, to transfer to Immaculate Heart of Mary. Again, it was his ability to speak Polish that helped to persuade the Diocese of Pittsburgh to permit the transfer.

The parishioners of Immaculate Heart of Mary immediately fell in love with their new associate priest. He was young, charismatic, charming, well-spoken, handsome, and athletic. He had grown up in the Polish Hill community, where his family still lived and everyone knew him while he was growing up. The elder Polish-speaking members of the congregation, for which there were many, loved the fact that they could speak with him in their native tongue. Besides,

Damian loved to be back home in Pittsburgh, where he was born and raised and where he grew up.

The duties of a Roman Catholic pastor of such a large parish were immense and sometimes daunting. In addition to administering the church's seven sacraments: baptism, confirmation, confession, holy communion, marriage, holy orders, and anointing of the sick pastor is responsible to preaching the Word of God and the truths of the faith; providing for Catholic education, especially for children and young people; fostering charitable works and social justice; and evangelizing the unchurched.

Immaculate Heart of Mary services 1,500 families with 5,000 parishioners. To assist Father Damian, the diocese of Pittsburgh had provided the Parish with two associate pastors. All three priests served to run the parish day-to-day operations. This also included running the elementary school, which provides education to children from first to eighth grades. Currently, Immaculate Heart of Mary school has an enrollment of 1,800 students, who are being taught by thirty Congregation of the Sisters of St. Joseph nuns and ten lay teachers. The school also employs a lay principal, three janitorial staff, and three cafeteria workers. The janitorial staff services both the church and school. Two secretaries and one nurse provided administration and health care support for the school. The cost to run both the church and school was immense. The tuition to attend the catholic school was barely enough to cover the cost to attend.

Although Polish Hill was not a wealthy area of Pittsburgh, the parishioners of Immaculate Heart of Mary were very generous with their weekly donations. Even these donations did not provide enough funds to pay for the upkeep and maintenance of the church. So the annual Polish festival was necessary to provide funds to help support both the school and church.

Father Damian also enjoyed the support of the local Council of the Knights of Columbus, North Hills Council #4029. When he first became Pastor, George Zanecky, the Grand Knight for this Council, offered the full support from the Knights to help with whatever Father Damian needed. Father Damian immediately took the opportunity to ask George and the Knights to help organize and run the Polish Festival fundraiser. Without hesitation, George agreed to serve as chairman for the 1960 Polish Day Festival.

Father Damian took an immediate liking to the young Grand Knight, and the two began to kindle a close friendship, which would eventually last their lifetimes. George and he were of the same age and, like Father Damian, was a charming and well-spoken man, known by his fellow parishioners as being a devout, humble Catholic. He was also an attorney who continued to live and work in Polish Hill, after graduating from law school. His skills as an attorney would serve him well in chairing the Polish festival committee. One of his duties would be to secure adequate insurance coverage and to obtain permits required by the City of Pittsburgh. Having contacts at City Hall would prove to be a huge advantage.

George soon found out that running this festival was much more than he had bargained for. The festival was originally organized as a one-day parish social event but eventually grew to a weekend event where the entire City of Pittsburgh was invited to attend. This year, it was decided to make it a weeklong event and to send invitation out to other Polish parishes located in the counties surrounding Pittsburgh, including those located in West Virginia and Ohio. The festival would include live demonstrations of Polish cooking, pierogi making, Polish pastries, hand-painted Polish Easter eggs, straw ornaments, Polish surname origins, Polish paper cuttings, St. Andrew's Eve fortune-telling, and a variety of Polish folk arts would be featured for festival guests to try, Polish folk songs, and the Polkas, Obereks, and Mazurkas from ten different Polka bands for the listening and dancing pleasure of attendees.

Contracts had to be obtained with vendors and musicians and permits obtained. For the first time, it was also decided to ask parishioners to open their homes for out-of-town attendees to live, free of charge. Lastly, the parish decided to purchase a block of tickets to the Pirates' doubleheader against the Cincinnati Reds on July 17. These tickets could be purchased on a first come, first served basis at a discount price.

The project was immense, and George needed to get started right of way. George had to solicit volunteers from both the Knights of Columbus and from parish members. The volunteers had to be interviewed and assigned to various subcommittees. He also needed to ask for volunteers who would be willing to open their homes and host people in need of accommodation free of charge.

After meeting with Father Damian, George walked to the front doors of the Immaculate Heart of Mary. He entered and knelt down and made the sign of the cross before entering the pew. He knelt down and looked at the tabernacle located behind the altar. It is in the tabernacle that Catholics believe God lived in the form of the sacred concentrated host. George reverently crossed himself and began to pray.

Chapter 14

The Committee

Pauline Pryzinski looked at herself in the vanity mirror and wondered how she had managed to get to look so old. There were bags under her eyes and crow feet around her eyes. She was only thirty-nine years old but looked and felt much older. The stress of dealing with an alcoholic husband was beginning to take its toll. She constantly worried that her husband was going to hurt himself or someone in the family while he was drinking. She began to contemplate leaving her husband and filing for divorce, but deep down, she knew that she loved her husband and wanted desperately to keep her young family together. Her Catholic faith and her belief in God were other driving force in her life to motivate her to try to deal best with what God had handed her with her husband's problems. Still, she was too proud to reach out for help and, up until now, made no effort to seek any type of legal, marital, or religious counsel. Her in-laws knew of the problems Peter was going through but stayed their distance, not wanting to interfere in their marriage. This made Pauline feel abandoned, and she knew that she was going to need to seek outside help eventually before it became too late.

She applied red lipstick, mascara, and rouge and was amazed at the transformation. She still was an attractive woman, she thought. She looked into her closet and pulled out a black-and-white dress with a pink bow near the white collar. She knew it was too nice to wear to her meeting, but tonight she wanted to look and feel pretty.

This would be the third meeting of the Polish Festival committee since Father Damien had invited her to join. Like the other meetings, her husband was working the late shift, so she didn't have to contend with his drunkenness. Pauline had not yet told her husband that she was on the committee and kept her attendance at these meetings a secret from him.

Pauline was becoming more comfortable with her role on the committee and enjoyed the relationship that she was forming with the rest of the committee members. She slid the dress over her head and pulled it down over her figure and smiled as the dress still fit her perfectly. The clock on her bedroom dresser read seven-fifteen. The meeting was scheduled to begin at seven-thirty, so she needed to hurry. The church was only a few blocks from her home, but she didn't was to be late. She grabbed a pair of high-heel shoes that she had bought for Easter. The heels hurt her feet, but she didn't care. They went well with the dress she was wearing and made her shapely legs look even more attractive.

She walked downstairs and found her three sons watching TV in the living. It was Wednesday evening, and the boys were watching their favorite western, *Gunsmoke*. They looked up at her in awe. They seldom saw their mother all dressed up outside of Sunday church or some other special occasion. "Where are you going, Mom?" Daniel asked. "You look great!"

She was still mad at both at her youngest and oldest boys for their baseball adventure, but somehow, Daniel always found a way to make her feel good. "Thank you," she said with a smile. "Have you boys finished your homework? Do you need me to check anything for you before I leave?"

The boys looked at her, saying nothing at first. Changing the subject, Michael asked again on behalf of everyone, "Where you going, Mom, all decked out?"

Pauline blushed, realizing that her appearance would make anyone question her intentions. "I have a meeting tonight of the Policy Festival Committee," Pauline responded. "I should be home no later than nine o'clock. I want you all in bed before I get home!" she demanded. "You father is working until midnight tonight."

The boys took little notice as to their father's work hours. It was always best to be fast asleep by the time he got home so that they didn't have to endure the fighting between their parents when he got home.

Pauline kissed all three boys, and the smell of her perfume lingered on their faces long after she had left the house. It was a clear but chilly May evening, and Pauline wished that she had worn something warmer. The brisk walk to Immaculate Heart of Mary Church helped to warm Pauline, but it also caused her feet to hurt, and she was now regretting wearing the high-heel shoes. The meeting was held in a small meeting room adjacent to the large hall in the basement. There were ten members of the committee, six men and four women. George Zanecky greeted her as Pauline walked into the conference room. "My, you look lovely tonight."

She was the last of the committee members to arrive and felt embarrassed as all eyes were on her. She quickly took a seat without saying a word to anyone. She felt uncomfortable with being in the spotlight, although her intentions all along were to make sure her wardrobe got everyone's attention.

"Okay, now that Pauline is here, we can get started," George said in an authoritative voice. Father Damien had placed George in charge of this committee, and as was his custom, George opened the meeting with a prayer. Pauline always marveled at George's ability to organize and run the meeting, something that she was that she could never do. Pauline had brought a notebook and pen and began taking copious notes. She wanted to make sure that she didn't miss anything and relied upon her notes to remind her afterward what was agreed upon and discussed in the meeting.

"As you are aware, we have received 250 responses to the invitations we sent up to the local Parishes before Easter. These individuals will be joining us at the Polish Festival in July and will be also going to the Pirates game that weekend. We have gotten over three hundred members of Immaculate Heart of Mary Parish to volunteer their homes for these out-of-town guests to stay while they are here in Pittsburgh for the festival. Tonight, we are going to match these guests with their host family."

With that being said, George walked over to the cage barrel they used to call Bingo and placed it on the table in from of the rest of the committee. "Inside this barrel are the names of the 250 individuals who are coming to the festival. Here is a list of all of our volunteer families listed in alphabetical name. We will call the name of the volunteer families first, then draw from the barrel the name of the individuals who they will be matched with." He looked at Pauline and handed her the list. "I need you to write down the names of the those chosen from the raffle barrel next to the families on this list," he said, smiling at Pauline as he handed her the list. "Once this selection process is completed, our job will be to send letters to each respective families advising each of whom they have been paired with. This is going to be a big job, so I hope everyone is up to the take. There are ten of us, so each will receive twenty-five individual families that we will have to write to. Does everyone understand before we get started?"

With no questions from the committee members, George began the selection process. Pauline worked hard to record the names onto her list as George pulled one name after another from the barrel. Pauline had volunteered their home to host but never told her husband. She decided to worry about that later as her name appears as the next to be assigned an attendee. George put his hand in the barrel and read the name. "Mr. Ben Brodziak from Windber, PA, and his eight-year-old son, Adam," George read as he handed the slip containing the Brodziak's name and address.

Pauline looked at the name and address. *Where is Windber, Pennsylvania?* she wondered. Adam Brodziak was the same age as her son Daniel. He would be going to a Pirates game with someone his own age. She only hoped that Adam liked baseball as much as her son did.

The selection process took longer than expected, and it was after nine by the time they were through. George distributed the list to all of the committee members with instructions to notify everyone on their list in writing and to have it done before their next committee meeting. The letters could be either handwritten or typed. Everyone was to keep track of the postage they used to mail the letters and then submit the receipt for reimbursement. George had a way of making things seem easier than they really were.

George and Pauline were the last two to leave the church. Pauline shivered as she walked into the chilly spring evening air. "Can I give you a ride, Pauline? I'm going right past your house."

Pauline looked surprised as she didn't realize that George even knew where she lived. By now, her feet were in agony, and she was not looking forward to walking the short distance back home. So, gratefully, she accepted George's invitation.

"I'm parked right over here," he said, pointing to a newer model Cadillac.

Wow, George must be doing pretty good for himself, she thought as he opened the passenger side door for her. She sat down on the seat and could feel and smell the leather interior.

"I just picked this up yesterday," George said as he got behind the driver's wheel.

"It's beautiful," replied Pauline, "I love the smell of a new car."

George pulled the Cadillac from the church parking lot and made a right turn in the direction of Pauline's home. The ride took all of a couple minutes as he pulled in front of the Pryzinski home. Pauline was hoping that her boys were in bed by now as she did not want them to see her getting out of this car. "I really want to thank you, Pauline, for all over your help," George said as he put the Cadillac in park and turned toward Pauline.

He was a very handsome man, she thought as she gazed into his eyes. "I'm glad to be of some help," she responded.

George looked at her without saying anything, and the awkward pause made Pauline feel uncomfortable while at the same time excited. She wondered what her life would have been like if she had married George instead of Peter. She ended the silence by saying goodnight. George remained silent as Pauline exited the car. He waved goodbye as he pulled away.

Pauline watched until the car disappeared in the distance. Her heart was racing, and she felt flushed as she walked to the front door of her home. She looked down at her dress and high heels and was glad that she had decided to get dressed up for the meeting. She was feeling good as she entered the house. It was dark and silent. She was grateful that the boys had gone to bed on time as she had instructed. Pauline sat on the living room couch in the dark and kicked off her heels. As she sat there in silence, she began to cry, wanting desperately to run away from her husband, her children, and her life. She began to pray as she did every night, seeking God's help to deal with the burden of her husband's drinking problem. Running away from this problem was not the answer.

Chapter 15

The Invitation

"Adam, can you run down to the mailbox and get the mail?"

Adam looked at his mother with apprehension. It had been raining all day, and he didn't feel like getting wet.

His father had purchased two acres of land from a local dairy farmer when Adam was in kindergarten. The land was located next to a dairy farm. During its heyday, the farm was home to over two hundred head of the finest dairy cows in Somerset County. Now the farm only housed about fifty head, but the farmer made a decent living selling milk from these cows. He was able to raise and milk the cows and pasteurize the milk right on the farm. He operated a small dairy store in town, where he was able to sell milk to the residence of Windber. Adam enjoyed living next to a farm because it gave him a sense of freedom, away from the town.

After purchasing the farm, his dad, along with his uncle, built a beautiful four-bedroom, two-story home, big enough to house their small family. The problem living here was that the home was located about a quarter mile from the main street on a hill overlooking the town below. The road had once been a service road to the farmhouse. The local post office would not deliver mail to an isolated home, located on top of a hill, which was hard to get to during the cold, snowy, wintery weather that western Pennsylvania was known for. So, in order to get their mail, the Brodziak family had to place their mailbox at the foot of hill, on main street, a quarter of a mile from the house.

Normally, his father would pick up the mail on his way home from work. Many times, it would snow while his father was a work, which would make it impossible to drive up the steep hill in his car. So often, his father would have to abandon the car and walk up the hill to their home. It was now May, so snow was not a problem. It had been and was still raining when his mother made her request of him to get the mail. Adam had planned to ask his mom's permission to go to the movies on Saturday. The local Arcadia Movie Theatre was playing a new Disney movie called *Swiss Family Robinson*, and he wanted to see the movie with his friends. His parents never let him go with his friends alone. He always had to go with his fourteen-year-old cousin, Polly. Adam felt that he was now old enough to go by himself. Retrieving the mail without complaining on this rainy day may be the thing he could do before asking her permission.

Adam had always loved to go to the movies at the Arcadia ever since he was a little kid. The Arcadia Theatre was built in 1920 and opened as a vaudeville house. Soon afterward, however, the theater was also showing silent and eventually sound pictures. The theater was located at the center of town and served on weekends as the sole entertainment for the small town. After the movies, moviegoers would visit Schaffer's drugstore located next door to treat themselves to ice-cream sundaes, soda floats, hamburgers, and candy. His cousin Polly loved to go there to listen to the jukebox and to try to meet boys. She always paid for what we ordered from money she got from his mother. It was now time for Adam to venture out on his own. Besides, *Swiss Family Robinson* was an adventure movie that his cousin probably wouldn't want to see.

Adam pulled on his black rubber galoshes; he hadn't worn them since the winter and, after placing his raincoat on, ventured out to get the mail. The rain was coming down hard by the time Adam got to the mailbox. He was soaked to the gills and still had to walk back up the hill to his house. He opened the mailbox and, without looking at it, placed the mail underneath his raincoat in hopes to keep in dry.

The round trip took about fifteen minutes. By the time he got into his house, he was dripping wet, cold, and miserable. His mother took one look at him and said nothing other than to take off his wet clothes. Adam began to wonder if it was worth the aggravation; did he really want to go to the movies that badly? Before taking off his coat, he opened it and gave the mail he was protecting to his mother. Surprisingly, the mail appeared to be completely dry, which made him feel very proud.

Adam watched as his mother opened the mail. He never took much notice to what the family received in the mail, but due to the efforts it took, he was interested in what was in the mail today. His mother looked at serval letters and placed them aside without opening any of them. "What is this?" she said suddenly, looking at the last of the letters. She puzzled over the envelope before deciding to open it. The return address was 34 Paulowna Street, Pittsburgh, Pennsylvania. Her family, as far as she knew, had no relatives or friends living in Pittsburgh. She had been their only once, on their honeymoon following their wedding. She tore open the envelope and retrieved the letter inside. The letter was addressed to her husband and was from someone named Pauline Pryzinski, and it read:

Dear Mr. Brodziak

My name is Pauline Pryzinski, and I am from Immaculate Heart of Mary Church in Pittsburgh, PA. I am also the Polish festival committee. As you know, our parish is holding its annual Polish festival on July 16th and 17th of this year. Earlier you expressed interest in attending this year's festival along with other interested members of your parish. As part of the celebration, we are also offering tickets at a discounted price for a double header between the Pittsburgh Pirates and the Cincinnati Red that will be played on Sunday July 17th.

At your request, we have reserved four tickets for this game. As a member of our Polish Day festival, I am also inviting you and your guests, at no charge, to stay at my home the weekend of

July 16th and 17th. The cost of transportation to my home is not included in this offer. I live at 34 Paulowna Street, Pittsburgh, PA, with my husband and three sons.

Please call me at TU4-6130, telegraph me, or write to me to confirm that you will be joining us this year. I look forward to hearing from you.

Sincerely,

Pauline Pryzinski

His mother looked a little perplexed as she laid the letter down on the countertop. "Who is the letter from?" Adam asked, followed quickly by, "Can I read it?"

Without saying a word, she gave the letter to Adam to read. It was then that she remembered that her husband spoke about attending this festival after reading about it in the Easter Sunday Church bulletin, but he never told her he was actually planning on going. She'd speak to him after he got home from work tonight.

Immediately after reading the letter, Adam asked his mother, "Mom, are we all going to Pittsburgh? Are we going to see a baseball game?"

His mother looked at him and smiled. "We'll see, son. I need to speak with you father first." Silently, she thought, *It would be nice to go away this summer. We haven't taken a vacation in years. I'd love to see Pittsburgh again, and it would be nice to meet new people.* Her husband would be home shortly, and she'd discuss it with him after dinner.

The thoughts about going to the movies this weekend left Adam's mind. Although he didn't like baseball, he knew that his dad would love to see a Pirates game, a doubleheader on top of that. Adam decided to wait on asking about going to the movies. His parents deciding on the invitation was far more important.

Chapter 16

The War

It was early Sunday morning when seventeen-year-old Peter Pryzinski awoke with a start and peeked out of his bedroom window. It was snowing heavily, which was a little unusual for this time of year, even for Pittsburgh. The snow combined with the smoke from the steel mills below made visibility very poor. The City of Pittsburgh was located in a valley, surrounded by hills, and located at the confluence of the Monongahela, Allegheny, and Ohio rivers. Many steel mills had been built along these three rivers. After Carnegie Steel was reorganized as US Steel in 1901, it and J&L Steel dominated the local economy of Pittsburgh in 1960. In addition to these giants, a number of smaller steel mills, refineries, and steel-fabricating factories were opened during the past century, making Pittsburgh, Pennsylvania, one of the largest steel-making cities in the world.

Along with the jobs they had provided, the steel industry also brought with it unbridled pollution. So it was not unusual for the area to be overcome with smog and soot. One would come out early in the morning to find their cars covered with a thin layer of sulfur dioxide emissions from mills which operated nonstop, with rare exceptions, seven days a week. Peter left school early in the eighth grade to work in the steel mills, following in the footsteps of his father and two older brothers. His father became ill with asthma from working too many years in the steel mills. Peter hated school and found working in the steel mills much more appealing for him.

The money was good, and his family could use the help now that his father was disabled.

Normally, Peter worked the night shift as did most of the younger unmarried employees. He normally also worked the weekends, including Sunday, which his mother did not like. She felt that a young boy his age needed to go to church on Sunday and not work. Regardless, the new guys were always given weekend shift, unless more senior men wanted the sift. So, on this cold December morning, Peter should be sleeping late, enjoying the day off. Instead, some ominous feelings swept over him, stirring him from a sound sleep. After lying in bed for thirty minutes, Peter could not fall asleep, so he climbed out of bed and walked downstairs.

His mother was in the kitchen, making coffee. "Your early," she said. "Do you want some coffee and breakfast? I can make you whatever you want." His mother was a good cook who fed her family of men really well. "Your father and brother are still sleeping, so first come, first serve."

"How about scrambled eggs and bacon, Ma? That would be swell," Peter replied. Peter opened the refrigerator, looked around inside, and retrieved a quart bottle of milk. For some reason, ice cold milk always helped to quench his thirst.

"Use a glass," his mother insisted.

Heeding her words, he opened the cabinet that held the glass cups. As he was pouring the milk, he looked at that calendar hanging on the wall. Today's date was Sunday, December 7, 1941.

It wasn't until later on in the day the City of Pittsburgh and the world learned about the Japanese surprise attack on the US Naval forces located at Pearl Harbor in Hawaii shortly in the morning, just before eight. The family all gathered around the Philco radio that his dad had purchased brand-new, just a year ago, to listen to news reports about the attack. The attack on Pearl Harbor took place before a declaration of war by Japan had been delivered to the United States. It was originally stipulated that the attack should not commence until thirty minutes after Japan had informed the US that it was withdrawing from further peace negotiations, but the attack began before the notice could be delivered.

Apparently, the entire Pacific fleet had been destroyed. It wasn't until the next day, December 8, 1941, that President Roosevelt proclaimed a formal Declaration of War against Japan. Congress quickly approved the Declaration of War, and so suddenly, America was in a war with Japan.

A demand for young men to join the armed forces to fight in the war immediately spread throughout the entire country. The City of Pittsburgh was no exception. Recruitment centers sprung up everywhere in the city. His oldest brother, Tom, was the first to enlist. He decided to join the Marines and was immediately given orders to report to Marine Corps Recruit Depot Parris Island in South Carolina. He would be leaving by the end of the week. His brother Stanley joined the army, and he, too, would be leaving within the week. His parents were completely distraught. Their world was being torn apart, and the future of their family was now in the hands of the US government, no longer in their control. Fortunately for them, Peter for now was too young to enlist. He wouldn't turn twenty-one for another four years, which was the age you had to be before a man could enlist. Maybe by then the war would be over, they naively thought. He would be safe at home until then.

Steelworkers had yet to be deemed essential to the war effort, so being a steelworker would not exempt them from being drafted, and the minimum age to voluntarily join was twenty-one; the government would eventually lower the minimum draft age to eighteen in 1942. Following the declaration of war, young men volunteered in droves to fight in the war and weren't about to wait to be drafted.

His mother kept all essential documents in a cedar hope chest that was located at the foot of their parents' bed. Included were her parents' marriage license and marriage certificate, baptism certificates, and birth certificates. Unsure what they would need to enlist, his mother had retrieved her son's birth certificates but demanded that they return them after enlisting. This would be the proof they could use to be able prove to the US government that both boys were twenty-one years of age.

Even though he was not yet old enough to join, Peter had another idea as to how he would enlist. After dinner that evening,

Peter snuck into his parents' bedroom while the rest of his family and huddled around the radio, listening to news about the war. Surprisingly, his mother had left the cedar chest unlocked. Ever since inheriting the chest from his grandmother, she had used the chest to hide away important documents and other cherished family heirlooms, so she never gave access to anyone, including his father. As Peter lifted the top of the cedar chest, he could smell the sweet aroma of cedar. According to his mother, cedar is a type of wood that naturally repels insects and fungus and proved to be an excellent place to store things of importance. The problem was that it made everything inside smell of cedar, which wasn't necessarily a bad thing.

Looking inside, Peter immediately began to search for his own birth certificate. Thinking it would be on top, he began to panic when he could not immediately locate it. Peter had not turned on the bedroom light in hopes of avoiding any suspicions from his family. So he had to begin digging harder, moving items aside in an effort to find his birth certificate. He had lifted each item up so he could see what he was looking at in the dim light he had available to him from the hallway light. He became frustrated as the search continued longer than he had originally intended. He was about to stop looking when his hand felt a piece of paper located at the bottom of the chest. He gently retrieved the document, taking care not to tear whatever he was holding. He lifted the document into the light. It read "birth certificate" along with his name, date, and place he was born. This is what he was looking for.

He quietly closed the lid, careful not to let anyone hear him. He immediately took his birth certificate to his bedroom, opened the bottom drawer of his dresser, and placed it underneath the clothes inside. He joined the family who gave no indication that they even knew he was not there. He would deal with his birth certificate later. For now, he just sat there, contemplating his next move.

*****

Early the next morning, Peter walked to the corner and took a bus, which would take him to Downtown Pittsburgh. He was heading for the Naval recruitment center located at South Craig Street. The ride would take him about thirty minutes, so it gave Peter plenty of time to contemplate what he was about to do. He was working the late shift tonight, and he told his mother that he was taking the bus this early to visit a sick friend to avoid any suspicions.

Before leaving, he had hastily retrieved his birth certificate from his dresser. The night before, he had found a pen in the junk drawer of the kitchen. While making certain no one was looking, he took the pen and used it to change the date of his birth on the certificate. It was a harebrained scheme, which he didn't think would work, but he desperately wanted to enlist. Forging his date of birth using a pen was the only idea he could think of. He was now twenty-one years of age and eligible to enlist to fight in the war.

It was 8:30 a.m. when the bus into Downtown Pittsburgh arrived at the corner bus stop. Peter jumped onto the bus, paid his fare, and found a seat near the front of the bus. It had snowed heavily the night before, but the streets were wet and clear of snow. He loved it when it snowed as it brightened the otherwise dreary Pittsburgh landscape. He felt underneath his winter coat where he was holding his birth certificate. He had been thinking long and hard about which branch of the service he wanted to join.

Ever since the war had started, the daily mail had been inundated with flyers from all branches of the Armed Forces, including the Coast Guard. His one brother had joined the Marines, the other the Army, so Peter felt the only other logical choice would be to join the Navy. "Men Make the Navy, and the Navy Makes Men" the pamphlet he was holding read. Peter knew nothing of the country of Japan, and as far as he knew, he never met a Jap. Now everyone wanted to kill the Japanese, and he was so no different. Since Japan had attached the Naval fleet at Pearl Harbor, the best way to take revenge was to join the Navy.

Peter continued to think of ways to hatch his plan to enlist in the Navy. Before he knew it, the bus suddenly came to a stop when he realized that they were in Downtown Pittsburgh. The bus driver called out, "South Craig Street," and jumped to his feet to exit from the bus. The tall building surrounded him causing him to become dizzy while he was looking upward.

After gaining his composure, Peter began to walk in the direction of the Naval Recruitment Center, which was only a short walk from the bus stop. When he found the front entrance, he walked inside, signed in at the front desk, and took a seat as he was instructed. The office was already busy this early in the morning with other young men eager to enlist. He was anxiously awaiting his turn when, finally, his name was called. He immediately got up, and he began to walk in the direction of the voice that had called his name. "Taken a seat, son," the man behind the desk said in a husky, authoritative voice. "Peter Pryzinski?" the man asked.

Peter looked at the man who was dressed in his Navy uniform. "Anthony Strong, Chief Petty Officer" his identification badge read.

"So you want to join the Navy?" Strong asked. "Do you know how to swim?"

Taken by surprise, the question made Peter realize that he had never learned to swim. It made sense that if he wanted to join the Navy, he would have to know how to swim.

"Relax, kid," Strong said, "I've been in the Navy ten years, and I still don't know how to swim. I was just kidding. Here, fill out these forms."

Peter relaxed, knowing that the Navy would not require him to know how to swim to join. Peter grabbed a pen and began completing the form. When it asked for his date of birth, Peter again panicked. He had forgotten the date he used when he changed it on his birth certificate. Turning his back to the recruitment officer, Peter retrieved the birth certificate from his coat. He returned to completing the form, using the new date he had used to change his date of birth. What seemed like forever, Peter finally completed the form and handed it back to the petty officer, who scanned it and after some questions, said to Peter, "Providing you pass the physical, looks like you're in. Welcome to the Navy."

A sense of relief passed over Peter as he began to rise from his seat to shake Strong's hand. Before he could get up, Strong said, "Oh, by the way, do you have your birth certificate?"

Peter's heart sank as he retrieved his birth certificate and handed it to the officer. Just then, someone called over, "Tony, we need your help over here right away."

Chief Petty Officer Anthony Strong quickly scanned Peter's birth certificate and handed it back to him. He signed the form that Peter had completed and returned it to Peter. "Welcome to the Navy," he said again, and the two men shook hands. Peter realized that he had just enlisted in the United States Navy but didn't yet know that he would soon be fighting the Japanese in the South Pacific.

Chapter 17

Love at First Sight

Peter received his basic training at the Great Lakes Illinois Naval training station located near North Chicago in Lake County, Illinois. Peter thought it was funny that he would have to train for seagoing warfare in the middle of the Midwest, far from any ocean. He soon found out, however, that training on the great lakes would be a different and grueling experience. Normally, basic training before the war began would last six months. Due to the wartime need for fighting men, the training period was compressed to two months.

Following his basic training, Peter was assigned to LCI(L) flotilla number 24. The Landing Craft Infantry (Large)—LCI(L)—was a large beaching craft intended to transport and deliver fighting troops, typically a company of infantry or marines, to a hostile shore once a beachhead was secured. He was ordered to Maryland Chesapeake Bay where he received training on board an LCI(L). LCIs were 158 feet long and twenty-three feet, three inches wide at the middle. They typically had a crew of twenty-four to sixty sailors and carried two hundred soldiers, who descended from ramps on each side of the craft during landings.

Once training here was complete, Peter was assigned to LSI(L)-1001 under the command of Lieutenant J. G. Richard Norton. Peter was flown by the Navy to San Diego, California, where he joined the ship's crew in May of 1944. Although he had not known it at the time, his ship and crew would be assigned to participate in the largest

Naval battle in the history of the world, a battle that would lead to the liberalization on the Philippines and the demise of the Japanese navy.

Because of its flat hull, the Navy classified the LCIL as a craft, not a ship. The flat hull allowed the LCI(L) to enter shallow waters with ease to deliver soldiers and equipment onto the beach. Unfortunately, its shallow hull also made it less than seaworthy, not fully designed for crossing large oceans like the Pacific Ocean. Its small size also caused the crew to become easily seasick from enduring bumpy waves during its long journey. So after joining its assigned convoy to cross the Pacific in August of 1944, Peter was amazed when he was the only one on board, including his commanding officers, who didn't get seasick.

This proved to be both a blessing and a curse for Peter. Because he never got sick, he had to take on extra duties while at the same time caring for the rest of the crew and the officers on board. It also endeared him to the crew and officers, making him the crew's favorite shipmate. There were twenty-five crew members, including himself and five officers, so when they landed in Hawaii to refuel, Peter was treated to many free beers, shots of liquor, and food while he was on liberty.

After refueling and before departing, the crew obtained their orders. Their convoy would leave Hawaii and join the main fleet under the command of Admiral William "Bull" Halsey somewhere in the Leyte Gulf near the Philippine Islands.

Over the summer of 1944, planes from the aircraft carriers of the US Third Fleet under Admiral William F. Halsey carried out several successful missions over the Philippines and found Japanese resistance lacking. Halsey then recommended a direct strike on Leyte Island, canceling other planned operations, and the Leyte invasion date set forward to October. They were to engage the Japanese fleet in Leyte Gulf and to make the way for an amphibious landing of Leyte Island. The entire joint forces of the Navy, Army, and Air Force was under the command of Army General Douglas J. MacArthur, who had previously promised the people of the Philippines that he would return, after being earlier ousted by the Japanese in May of

1941. The responsibility of the Twenty-Fourth LCIL flotilla in this campaign would be to reinforce and resupply, provide anti-aircraft and security support, and serve as rescue and salvage.

The Battle of Leyte Gulf began at dawn on October 17, 1944. The invasion of Leyte Island followed shortly on October 20, 1944. By 13:30, on the twentieth, enough of the island had been secured to allow General MacArthur to make a dramatic entrance through the surf, onto Red Beach, and announce to the populace the beginning of their liberation: "People of the Philippines, I have returned! By the grace of Almighty God, our forces stand again on Philippine soil."

During the battle, LCI(L)-1001 quickly went into action, attempting fanatically to recue drowning and wounded men from the water. Peter and two of his crew entered a life raft and began to row in areas close to their ship in an attempt to save the men floating in the water. Peter pulled one man after another into the raft. As best as possible efforts were made by his team to care for their wounds. The raft was nearly full, and they were about to return to their ship, when Peter spotted a man floating nearby. "They're one more guy over here," he called to his crew.

Immediately, they began to row the raft to the area where Peter was pointing. As the raft pulled alongside, Peter reached down to pull the man aboard the raft. As he tried to lift him, Peter continued to encourage the man in hopes of soliciting a response but received none. With all his might, Peter lifted the man into the raft. To his horror, the man was dead, torn in half at the waist with both his arms missing. He was also Japanese.

During the battle, Japanese fighter pilots appeared to have been attacking the fleet by intentionally dive-bombing into unsuspecting ships in what would be later known as suicide or Kamikaze bombing. Holding the dead man in his arms, Peter realized that, although the Japanese were the enemy. They were men like him who left their wives, children, family, and friends to fight for their country. This man would never see them again. This incident, along with many more Peter witnessed during the war, would go on to haunt him for the rest of his life.

The war ended, following the surrender of the Japanese on September 2, 1945. Peter was discharged from the Navy shortly afterward in San Francisco California, where the fleet returned shortly after peace was declared. Peter took a train from San Francisco back to Pittsburgh where he was met at the train station by his mother, father, and two brothers, both of whom had also survived the war. His brother Tom was severely wounded in the Battle of Iwo Jima and would never return to action, and Stanley managed to survive both D-Day and the Battle of the Bulge. Both his mother and father looked much older than when he first left for the war, but he had never seen them look happier. They would all later tell their own war stories, but for now, they were all home again, safe and sound, and home again. Peter had left Pittsburgh, a boy of seventeen, and was returning a young man, eager to get back to work and start his life over again.

They drove from the train station to their home on the Polish Hill section of the city. Peter was quiet during the ride home, taking in the sights of the city, wondering how long it would take him to reacquaint himself to civilian life. His dad parked the car in front of the house. His brother had already been home for a while before Peter and they ran ahead up the steps of the home. Peter paused as he got out of the car and looked around. The three domes of Immaculate Heart of Mary Church loomed in the background like a sentinel for the community. Peter couldn't remember the last time he had been at Mass. He was never much of a religious person, and even during the war, he never attended services, even though he prayed to God every day to help bring his home from the war.

When he entered the house, he could smell the sweet aroma of his mother's Polish cooking. His mother had planned a welcoming home party for the boys and had invited all of their relatives, most of whom lived in or around Polish hill. They would be arriving soon to greet the returning warriors. Peter was not looking forward to their small party but knew it meant everything to his parents for all the family to get together. After finishing the meal of traditional Polish food, perogies, Gołąbki, potato pancakes, bigos, and paczki for dessert. The family all gathered in the living room, where they laughed and drank bottles of Iron City beer. His brothers had no desire to share their war stories with the family, so most of the conversation centered around what had happened with the family after they had left for the war. So Peter learned who in the family got married and to whom, who was pregnant, or would have given birth. Many of the men in the family worked in the steel mills, so plans were being made to get the boys their old jobs back. Around midnight, the last of the partygoers left.

Peter was alone with his mom in the kitchen. He had always sensed that he was his mother's favorite, although she never let on. "Mom, I'm tired," Peter said and kissed her on the forehead. His mother reached over and gave him a big hug. "Immaculate Heart of Mary Church is having a welcoming home party this coming weekend. Why don't you go? There will be a lot of pretty single girls." She said it in an enticing way. "Maybe, Mom, but right now I need to get some sleep."

Saturday morning, Peter woke up early. He had not yet unpacked his Navy duffel bag, which contained the last mementos of his last four years' service. Inside he found the uniform which the Navy allowed him to take home, including his white sailor's cap. He would find a way to preserve this uniform, so some day, his kids would see what he wore while in the Navy. Peter received three campaign medals the Navy had awarded him following his participation in the battle of Leyte Gulf, and for action he saw at Mindanao Island, and Sulu Archipelago. He was proud of these medals as they reminded him of the sacrifices he and his crew had made during the war. He placed them gently inside his bedroom dresser under the civilian clothes that he left behind after he joined the Navy.

After unloading his duffel bag, he walked downstairs to get breakfast. The rest of the family were all awake, enjoying stacks of pancakes, and scrambled eggs. Before he could even say good morning, his brother Tom grabbed him, saying, "Are you going to the party tonight, little bother? It's going to be lots of fun and even better lots of girls." Peter remembered that his mother had earlier told him about the party, but he hadn't thought about it since.

406

"The church has spent a long time planning this party," his mother chimed in. "You boys should all go," she recommended. The party was scheduled to begin at 8:00 p.m. in the church hall located in the basement of Immaculate Heart of Mary Church. All returning servicemen from the Parish were being invited. There would be plenty of food, beer, and wine and a live big band ragtime orchestra would be providing the dancing music. Peter hadn't been to Immaculate Heart of Mary Church since he left Catholic School there in the eighth grade, and he was feeling uncomfortable about going back after all these years. After nonstop coaxing from his bothers and mother, he finally agreed to attend, especially after he learned that servicemen were invited to come to the party dressed in uniform. It would be nice for him to show off his uniform to the neighborhood.

Peter looked in the mirror and thought, *It still lifts.* He had gained weight since he was discharged from the Navy, but his uniform still fit. He placed his white sailors cap on his head and turned it slightly in accordance with Naval uniform regulations. He still had mixed feelings about going to tonight's party. For some reason, he felt too old to attend. His brothers, however, were really gung-ho and couldn't wait to show off their respective military uniforms. Peter suspected that they were more interested in meeting girls tonight than anything else. After serving four years in wartime service for their country, most men were more than ready to meet someone, settle down, get married, have kids, and raise a family. Peter had no such desire to meet anyone. He was a shy guy and was never one to be a ladies' man. For now, the only thing he wanted to do was to get his old job back at the steel mill and to start making money.

With most of the rest of the world being devastated by the bombing and invasions of their countries, few had the manufacturing capabilities to rebuild. The United States survived the war, totally unscathed and fully intact, with full manufacturing capabilities to help rebuild the rest of the world. Because of this, the United States experienced unprecedented economic doom, which meant that there was plenty of jobs available for the young servicemen returning from the war, so Peter planned to take advantage and get back to work as soon as possible. He wanted to earn enough money to buy his own

91

house. He also wanted to remain free of any burdens, including marriage, that would stand in his way.

It was a little after 8:00 p.m. when Peter left the house and began walking to Immaculate Heart of Mary Church. The church was only several blocks up the hill from his parents' home. His brothers had left earlier, so Peter was all along as he trudged up the hill. His anxiety grew the closer he got to the church. He did not know what to expect, and his feet felt like lead as he opened the door to the church basement. He was immediately engulfed with the sights and sounds associated with a large party atmosphere. The din of the music, dancing and talking made it impossible to think, and he immediately began feeling regret in coming. Peter looked around and could not find anyone he remembered or knew, when suddenly he was pushed from behind. He turned to see both his brothers, each holding a girl in hand, greeting him.

"Girls, I want you to meet my little brother, Pete. Pete, meet Florence and Carol."

Peter nodded and shook both of their hands. "Pleasure to meet you," he responded. "Watch out for these two brutes. They're up to no good tonight."

His brother Tom slapped him on the back of his head, almost causing him to lose his sailor's cap. "Come on, brother, let's try to get you to meet some girls." Peter felt embarrassed as his brothers began to push him through the crowded basement. Peter looked around, and for the first time, he noticed the large number of servicemen who were in attendance. Judging by their uniforms, all branches and ranks of the military seemed to be widely represented. Suddenly, Peter felt a great sense of pride in himself and was glad that he was there, representing the US Navy. He began to wonder where they had served during the war and what battles they had fought. He decided that he would walk around and try to speak with these men to get more information from them about their experience in the war.

A table of food and refreshments was set up on the far side of the hall, where a handful of young women were offering help to serve people coming up to the table. His brothers and their female acquaintances pushed Peter toward the table. "Let's get something to eat and drink first."

Tom said, "I think the punch is spiked from the taste of it."

Peter did not like the taste of either beer or liquor and seldom drank much, even when he was at liberty during the war. He also wasn't hungry, but wanting nothing more than to appease his brother so that they would get out of his hair, Peter stood in line in front of the table.

As he stood in line, Peter immediately noticed a beautiful young girl standing across the table, serving punch to those waiting in line. He couldn't take his eyes off of her and wondered who she was. As Peter got closer to the punch bowl, and as he began to wonder what he would say, he immediately recognized her; she was Pauline Piatek. The two of them were in the same grade school class at Immaculate Heart of Mary, but Peter had not seen her since dropping out of school in the eighth grade. She had grown up to be a beautiful woman, with golden blonde hair and with a gorgeous womanly figure. It was like love at first sight, if anyone can believe in such a thing. As he approached and before he could say anything, Pauline called out to him, "Peter Pryzinski, is that really you?" Pauline immediately left her post behind the punch bowl, went around the table, and gave Peter an unexpected big hug. She kissed him on the cheek, then pulled away. "Look at you, you look so handsome in your uniform. I was hoping you would come. I saw your mom last Sunday at Mass, and she told me you would be back in time for this party. I'm glad you came." She kissed him again on the cheek.

Peter was dumbfounded. He didn't even think that she even knew he existed, let alone hoping they would meet again after all these years. "I'm glad to see you again, Pauline," he said sheepishly, not knowing what else to say. How could this beautiful woman have any interest in him?

"Wait five minutes. My shift will be over, and we can talk more," she said.

Before he knew it, he and Pauline were together embarrassing one another as they danced on the dance floor. She was beautiful and smelled so good. She would not stop talking as they danced, but

Peter didn't care. She made him feel so much at ease, like they had been together all of their lives. Once the band stopped playing for a break, Peter offered, "Do you want to go outside where it's a little quieter?"

"Yes," she said with an unexpected degree of enthusiasm, "let me get my sweater."

Although it was early spring, the weather was unusually warm for this time of year. As they left the church hall, Pauline grabbed his hand. Peter blushed, not expecting that she would want to hold her hand. The City of Pittsburgh had installed a bench on the sidewalk, underneath a streetlight. They walked slowly toward the bench and sat down. "I've been thinking about you, Peter, ever since I heard that you had enlisted in the Navy and went to fight in the war. I prayed the rosary every day since then, hoping that God would bring you home safely," she said. "I thought about writing to you but thought better of it as word got around that the military was discouraging people other than the immediate father from sending letters. The claim was for national security."

"I'm sorry about that," Peter said, not knowing what else he could say. "I didn't even know you liked me, Pauline. It's been so long since we've been in school together."

"I've always liked you, Peter, ever since the fourth grade, when you gave me a Valentine's Day card," Pauline responded.

Peter couldn't recall. The best he could remember, he would give everyone in class a Valentine's Day card. He was glad she remembered, however, as he moved closer to her on the bench. Mustering enough courage, he placed his arm around her shoulders, pulling her closer to his body. She immediately obliged and was grateful to be in his arms. Unaccustomed as he was to any form of intimacy, especially from a woman, he suddenly felt at ease and unafraid of showing his emotions. He began to talk to Pauline in a way that he had never spoken to anyone in his life.

He began to tell Pauline everything about his life since they last saw one another. From his days working in the steel mills before the war, to how he forged his birth certificate and the time he had spent in the Navy from basic training to his experience in the South

Pacific, fighting the Japanese. Before he knew it, an hour had gone by as he looked at Pauline sitting next to him. She appeared to be in a trance, looking at him in amazement and longing. "I love you, Peter Pryzinski," she said and leaned over and kissed him on the lips.

Chapter 18

Just One More Drink

Peter quickly learned that being in love with a woman completely changed a guy's outlook on life. The future plans he had set for himself no longer mattered. Shortly after the welcoming home party, he and Pauline started dating. For their first date, Peter had invited her to join him for breakfast at Kaibur Coffee and Café, which was a small local Polish deli located on Polish Hill. The deli served the best coffee and breakfast and was a nice place for a couple to meet and talk. Following this first date, they agreed to meet there every Saturday morning at eight-thirty. They would spend hours just talking about everything from family and friends, the war, religion, and their personal likes and dislikes. These talks helped them to grow to know and understand one another.

Peter had learned that after graduating from high school, Pauline attended the St. Margaret School of Nursing in Pittsburgh. She had to drop out after two years because her parents could no longer afford the tuition. She was, however, able to earn an LPN degree, and got a job at the Corner View Nursing and Rehabilitation Center as a nursing assistant. The pay wasn't great, but she enjoyed the work, helping the elderly patients with their rehabilitation and care. Peter recalled that Pauline was always a very bright and ambitious student while attending grade school at Immaculate Heart of Mary, so a career in nursing appeared to be appropriate for her.

Pauline still lived with her parents and two younger sisters, whose home was just around the corner from Peter's home. Her parents had immigrated from Poland to Pittsburgh in 1909. Because they spoke Polish as their primary language, Pauline learned through them to speak and read Polish. Having no brothers, her parents avoided the pain, heart attacks, and concerns brought about by World War II. Regardless, the entire family had dedicated hours of volunteer work to help the war relief efforts, and they were just as equally happy as those who had sons, when the war ended.

Pauline was also a very devout Catholic, who attended Mass at Immaculate Heart of Mary almost every day when possible. So as their relationship grew, Pauline began to invite Peter to go back to church. Peter was reluctant at first since he hadn't been to church is a very long time after he left Parochial school in the eighth grade and didn't consider himself to be a religious person. Although she never pushed him, Pauline's religious influence began to rub off on Peter. While walking back home, after attending a movie one Saturday afternoon, Pauline asked, "Peter, will you go with me to Mass tomorrow?"

Peter was taken aback. He wasn't sure that God would accept him back to the church after all these years. "It's been so long since I've been to church," he said. "Do you think it would be okay to come back?"

Pauline giggled and replied, "Of course, silly, you're always welcome to come to church."

He's probably had to go to confession first before he could receive Holy Communion, she thought, but for right now, Pauline didn't want to press the issue any further with him. *First things first*, she thought, *let me get him back to church first, then we could talk about going to confession.*

"If that's what will make you happy, then okay," Peter promised. Without saying a word, Pauline stopped, turned to Peter, stood on tiptoes, and gave him a kiss. She felt light as a feather. She was afraid that he would refuse ever to return to church again, and no matter how much she loved him, she could never marry a man who was not a practicing Catholic.

The next day, they decided to attend the 10:00 a.m. Mass at Immaculate Heart of Mary. Peter met Pauline at the front steps of the church, dressed in the only suit he owned. He was extremely nervous until he saw Pauline walking on the sidewalk, approaching the church. She looked beautiful as always. She wore a square-shouldered jacket with simple blouses and a matching skirt with matching blunt-toe box shoes, decorated with a pink bow. To him, she looked like an angel. His nervousness disappeared as soon as she grabbed his arm and gave him a kiss.

"You look handsome, Peter," she said, "I love your suit." He knew that she must have been kidding him about the suit but didn't care as they walked up the steps to the front entrance of the church.

Peter stopped before going inside. The last time he had gone to Mass at this church was when he received his confirmation in the eighth grade, and in fact, that was the last time he had attended Mass anywhere since then.

"It'll be all right," Pauline encouraged as she led him into the church.

Peter entered and looked around. It looked the same since he was last there. Immaculate Heart of Mary was designed and built in the style of the cathedrals that were hundreds of years old in Poland. Although the exterior of the church was a beautiful landmark, it was the interior that was truly amazing. The dome in the middle of the church contained clear glass windows which provided nature sunlight for the interior of the church. There were twelve marble columns that supported the roof of the church. The main aisle led from the front of the church to a beautiful ornate altar, which housed the tabernacle. Catholics believed that the living body of Jesus Christ resided in the tabernacle in the form of the consecrated host. In front of the altar was the Communion railing, where parishioners knelt to receive Holy Communion. Pews lined each side of the main aisle, where Mass attendees would sit during Mass. The church was large enough to hold 1,500 people and was one of the largest Catholic churches in the City of Pittsburgh.

Pauline stopped to place a veil over her head, which was customarily a sign of reverence for women who were attending Mass.

Men were required to remove their hats. Fortunately for Peter, he didn't wear one today, due to the fact that he did not even own a hat. Peter looked around the church as Pauline guided the couple to the front pews of the church. Before entering the pew, Pauline knelt down, and made the sign of the cross. Genuflecting is a reverence to express adoration of the blessed sacrament contained on the altar.

Peter was still looking around the church and hadn't taken notice and almost tripped over Pauline as she was genuflecting. Peter made a half-hearted effort to kneel and make an awkward sign of the cross before sitting next to Pauline in the pew. She had chosen a pew near the front of the church, which made Peter feel a bit uneasy. He wondered if Pauline had done that to bring him closer to the action once the mass began.

The ringing of bells along with the organ and choir singing marked the beginning of the mass. The ten o'clock mass at Immaculate Heart of Mary Church was always a High Mass, which is full of ceremonials including acolytes, a censer with license, and a choir, and which always lasted longer than a normal Sunday Mass. With the exception of the gospel, Sunday Mass was always said in Latin. As the Mass proceeded to the reading of the gospel, known as the "Liturgy of the Word," Peter watched as the priest placed incense inside the censer, being held by the altar server. Immediately the church exploded with the strong odor of burning incense. Since they were so close to the altar, the smell of incense was exceptionally strong where they were sitting. Even though it made Peter's eyes water, he found that he rather enjoyed the smell.

The priest celebrating Mass today was Father Ronald Dansky. Peter would later learn that Father Ron had been ordained a year earlier and assigned to Immaculate Heart of Mary Parish. Peter observed as Father Ron took the censer containing the incense and slowly encircled the ambo holding a large Bible, embossed with gold writing on the front cover. Once Father Ron completed this ceremony, he walked to the ambo and recited, "Dóminus vobíscum."

The entire congregation responded, "Et cum spíritu tuo," while making the sign of the cross on the Bible.

Father Ron recited the Latin words "Glória tibi, Dómine."

The congregation responded by crossing themselves with their thumb on the forehead, lips, and chest. When he was in grade school, Peter's parents insisted that be become an altar boy. He quit shortly afterward because he couldn't remember the Latin words that were required. Listening to the words spoken in Latin today at this Mass reminded Peter that he never got to know what they meant. Peter wondered if Pauline or anyone else at Mass today knew what they meant.

Following the reading of the today's gospel, which was from John 6:35, Father Ron gave a brief homily addressing today's gospel reading. He explained that this gospel was known as the Bread of Life Gospel. In this gospel, Jesus declared, "I am the bread of life. Whoever comes to me will never go hungry, and whoever believes in me will never be thirsty."

Father Ron tried to explain, "Jesus is saying that ultimately, he can satisfy our deepest needs and longings. He can make us feel full and overflowing with blessing."

Peter looked at Pauline as the priest spoke these words and thought how blessed he was that she had somehow managed to come into his life and realized how much he really loved her. Peter wondered, *Has God brought the two of us together through his divine intervention?* He would learn just how important she would become to him later on in his life.

Peter began attending Mass every Sunday and, with Pauline's guidance, began going to confession and receiving Holy Communion. As a result, the two grew closer and closer and soon became inseparable. Peter regained his old job at the steel mill and was working long and hard hours. Pauline became his one and only desire in life, and he knew that he would soon be asking for her hand in marriage. Every penny he made went into his marriage savings account. He not only wanted to have enough money to afford an engagement ring but wanted to also be able to buy a house where they would live. So he decided that he was going to propose to her on Christmas Day.

As was the Polish custom, the families met for a traditional Christmas Eve celebration which was a day first of fasting, then of feasting. The Wigilia feast begins at the appearance of the first star.

His mother served a cod fish dinner along with many other traditional Polish dishes and desserts. Following the dinner meal, Peter and Pauline walked to Immaculate Heart of Mary Church to attend Midnight Mass. It was a cold evening, and snow began to fall just as the two entered the church. The Christmas Mass was long but beautiful, heralded by Polish Christmas carols and a procession around the church by the grade school children. The lights in the church were turned off and replaced by light from hundreds of beautiful Christmas lights. The front altar contained six twenty-foot Christmas trees, all of which were ornately lit and decorated. Six inches of newly fallen snow greeted the parishioners as they left Mass.

The couple felt like kids as they skated down the icy, snowy sidewalks of Polish Hill to Pauline's house. As they walked onto the front porch of the house, Peter could hardly contain himself with excitement. He had picked up the engagement ring from Polski's Jewelers earlier in the week. It cost him three months' salary to buy the half-carat diamond ring, but it was worth it. He examined the ring almost constantly afterward, proud of his selection. Before leaving for Mass, Peter had hidden the ring in the suit jacket and was constantly obsessing over its safety. All he needed was to lose the ring now, right before he proposed.

The snow was coming down harder, and a beautiful white overcoat painted the surrounding city. *What a perfect night to propose marriage*, he thought as he pulled the ring from its hiding place. Holding the ring in his right hand, he turned to Pauline and got down on one knee. She looked like an angel illuminated by the dim glow of Christmas lights, her father had used to decorate the front porch. The white snow flurrying around her face added to her elegance. She gasped as he opened the box in front of her, and he nervously asked, "Pauline Piatek, will you marry me?"

She grabbed the ring from his hand and placed it on her finger. "Yes, Peter, oh yes, I'll marry you!," Pauline said as she pulled him to his feet. She kissed him and said, "I love you, Peter Pryzinski. I'll always love you!"

It was Christmas Day 1947, the beginning of the next chapter in Peter's life. He had survived the war and now stood together with his beautiful wife-to-be. He felt blessed again as he stood there, silently thanking God for what he had just given him.

The two got married in August the following year during a hot Pittsburgh day. They decided not to take a honeymoon but instead used the money they saved to buy a house on 34 Paulowna Street in Polish Hill. Shortly after getting married, Pauline got pregnant, with their first child, Michael. Over the course of the next five years, they would have two more boys, Luke and Daniel. Pauline continued to work at the nursing home but left after Daniel was born, to raise her family full-time. The economy was booming, as was the steel industry, so Peter always had work, making great steelworker wages. Life was good for the Pryzinski family.

One night, as they were sleeping in their bed, Pauline was awoken by the loud screams coming from her husband who was lying close by. Peter appeared to be still asleep but was tossing and turning as he screamed. "Peter, honey, wake up! What's the matter! Are you alright?," she asked.

Peter awoke with a start, sitting straight up; he was sweating, and his pajamas were soaked with perspiration. He could hardly breathe as he attempted to regain his composure. He turned to Pauline, still sobbing, and said, "He has no arms! He has no arms!"

"Who has no arms, Peter?" she replied but got no response.

Peter appeared to be in a trance, not recognizing his wife. "He has no arms," he continued to say over and over again. Finally, and while still sobbing, Peter fell back to his pillow and fell asleep. Pauline didn't know what to do and decided against trying to reawaken him for fear he would resume his rants. She decided to try to talk to him the next morning about what had happened.

*****

The next morning, when she approached him, he denied having any knowledge of what had happened to him the night before. "Must have been a bad dream, that's all," Peter said dismissively. Pauline showed no concern initially, but these nightmares became a nightly occurrence. Every time, Peter would deny having any recollection. Pauline did not know what to do. It was not customary and even frowned upon to seek help from anyone outside the immediate family, so Pauline remained silent about her husband's dreams.

One day after work, the men on Peter's crew invited him to go with him to a local Polish Falcons Club for a drink. They invited him every day after work, but Peter always refused. He loved to get home in time to enjoy having dinner with his family. His boys were getting older, and he wanted to make sure he was home in time before they went to bed. Besides, he was never much of a drinker. Even in the Navy, Peter would seldom drink while on liberty. "Pauline's expecting me to be home for dinner today," he said.

"Come on, Pete, just one drink won't kill you to have with your buddies," one in the crew responded. Peter had not been feeling himself recently and, for the past several months, began feeling anxious and depressed. Maybe one drink would help him get over it, so Peter broke down and agreed. "Just one drink won't hurt. I'll be home in plenty of time for dinner."

Every time he tried to leave the bar that night, one of his crew challenged him, "Just one more drink, Pete, then go home." The group had entered the bar around 4:30 p.m. after their shift had ended. Peter never got home that night until well after midnight. He was so drunk when he got home that he could hardly stand. This would become a daily occurrence for Peter, something that would repeat itself for many years to follow.

Chapter 19

The Pennant Race

The *Pittsburgh Press* daily newspaper had been delivered to the Pryzinski home earlier than usual today, which gave Daniel the opportunity to grab the sports section before the rest of the family got a hold of the paper. The newspaper was dated Wednesday June 1, 1960. The Pirates had beaten the Cincinnati Reds the night before, 5 to 0, which gave them a game and a half lead over the San Francisco Giants in the National League standings. Although Daniel knew the Pirates had won, the game was broadcast that evening, too late for Daniel to stay up and listen. His last day of school was on Friday, which meant that he could stay up late the entire summer to listen to the games on the radio. For now, he had to be satisfied with reading the box score in the newspaper baseball section.

Bob Friend was the winning pitcher for the Pirates and now possessed a pitching record of 6–2. More importantly, Friend had pitched a nine-inning shutout, giving up only three hits and one base on balls. Friend was quickly becoming the Pirates' ace. Looking at the box score, Daniel noted first that the Pirates had scored 5 runs on 11 hits. The top of the lineup, Hoak, Groat, Shinner, and Nelson had two hits apiece. Clemente had only one hit, a triple, which had driven in two of the Pirates' five runs. He also led the team with a batting average of .350. Moving down the box score, Daniel noted that his favorite player, second baseman Bill Mazeroski, was batting in the lowly 8 batting spot, just above the pitcher. Although Bill had gotten a hit in the game, he was off to a slow start for the beginning of the season and was only hitting for a .225 average. Regardless, the Pirates had won and were in first place, which was all Daniel cared about for the moment.

"Daniel Pryzinski, you're going to be late for school if you don't stop reading that paper," his mother warned.

Daniel didn't really care; it was the last week of school for the year, so there wasn't much they were doing anyway. He laid the newspaper down and grabbed his schoolbooks. "Don't throw the sports page away," he yelled to his mother as he left the front door. "I haven't finished reading the box score from yesterday's game." This was a lie, which didn't fool his mother, but after any Pirates win, Daniel always loved to read the box score over and over again. By doing this, it enabled him to relive the game in his mind, as though he had actually been there.

It was an exciting time of year for young Daniel. School was ending for the summer, and the Pirates were in the midst of a pennant race. What could be better? He only wished that his parents would get along better. It was hard for him to see his father struggling with his drinking problems, but being only eight years old, there was nothing he could do, which made him feel helpless. He was starting to become withdrawn and had little friends he could talk to. Baseball had become the one thing he could count on and had become his escape from worrying about his dad. The Pittsburgh Pirates baseball team players became his friends. He concluded that if nothing changed in his life, baseball would always be there as his a source of comfort.

Daniel ran up the sidewalk toward Immaculate Heart of Mary Church and the adjacent Catholic school building. Sister Mary Agnes greeted him as he entered the classroom. Most of the class was already seated, so Daniel felt a little uncomfortable being the last one. Even though Sister said nothing to him about being late, he didn't like being the center of attention. "I will be passing out your final report cards on Friday," Sister said as she began the class.

Getting your final report card was always a stressful time of year for a grade school kid. Those students with failing grades would have to repeat the grade, which to everyone was the ultimate embarrassment. Could you image having to repeat the fourth grade, when all of the rest of the class moved on to the fifth grade? Daniel didn't want to think about it. He was a good student and had gotten good grades all year long, so he wasn't worried about flunking. His brother Mike told him that he thought that his friend, Jay Dinger, would likely have to repeat the eighth grade. Even though Daniel thought Jay was a jerk, he still felt bad for the guy if he was going to fail the eighth grade.

"So let's talk about what you students plan on doing this summer?" Sister asked. One by one, each of these classmates raised their hands to take turns to answer Sister's question. Daniel hadn't thought much about his summer plans. His parents never took the family anywhere on vacation. He was still too young to work, even as a paperboy. So when it was his turn, Daniel said the only thing that made sense to him. "I want to go see the Pirates play baseball this summer."

He felt a little embarrassed by his answer but felt a sense of relief when Sister acknowledged his plan as being a noble one. "They're having a great season so far," Sister said. "I'd like to see them play as well. Maybe we could go together." she exclaimed as the rest of the class laughed. He wouldn't be caught dead going to a game with his teacher, let alone a nun. She pointed at a poster that was hanging on the wall near the chalkboard. "Don't forget about our annual Polish festival this summer," she reminded the class. "Daniel, maybe your dad will take you to the doubleheader baseball game. Don't forget the Parish has purchased tickets for the game that they will be selling as part of the festival."

This was the first time Daniel had heard of these tickets. He looked closer at the poster which provided him with more details. As part of the festival, the Parish was offering tickets to the Pirates scheduled doubleheader with the Cincinnati Reds on Sunday July 17. Daniel became excited at the prospect of seeing a doubleheader and wondered how he could mention this to his parents. Although his dad preferred to watch the Steelers play football, maybe he would consider taking his sons to a Pirates game instead. His enthusiasm waned as he realized that his dad had never taken any of his sons to a baseball game, and that it would be highly unlikely for him to do so now. Daniel silently hoped maybe with the Pirates playing so well, this season, maybe his dad would go.

The morning classes—math, English, and catechism—were taught with the same vigor by Sister Mary Agnes and with the same demand for participation like it was for the first day of school. Daniel had hoped that the last several days of the school year were going to be easy for him and his classmates. Daniel should have known better. Sister Mary Agnes had a reputation for being a taskmaster. She didn't want to leave her class before imparting on them all the last bits of knowledge she could before they graduated to the fifth grade. It took every ounce of willpower for Daniel to concentrate on what was being taught. So, when class recessed for lunch, Daniel was the first one to get up to go to the lunchroom. Before doing so, he walked over to the poster hanging on the wall to make sure he gathered as much information regarding the Polish Festival as he could, especially the part regarding the tickets for the doubleheader on July 17.

Apparently, the parish had purchased a bulk of tickets from the Pirates that they in turn could sell or give away as part of the Polish Festival celebration. The Pirates were going to honor the Immaculate Heart of Mary Church during the doubleheader with the Reds on the 17th. This looked like a big deal to Daniel. The poster announced that there were only four tickets available for each family wanting to attend. The Parish was also going to raffle off four tickets to the game. The raffle tickets would be sold for $1 each. Daniel thought that it would be great if his family purchased four tickets, then he could go to the game with his dad and two brothers.

During lunch, Daniel ran into his older brother, Michael, and presented the information about the doubleheader to him. "Mike, what about asking Mom and Dad if they could purchase tickets for the family? Dad would listen to you more than me," Daniel asked.

"I already know about the tickets. Didn't you know that Mom's on the Polish Festival committee. She's been planning this thing for a couple of weeks already," Mike responded. "She knows all about the tickets, but I'm not too sure if she's crazy about asking Dad if it would be okay with him. You know how he could be about spending money." Daniel never thought of his father as being a spendthrift, but he could read between the lines. His mother likely didn't want to ask him for fear that he couldn't remain sober long enough to sit through a doubleheader. Regardless, Daniel made up his mind that he was going to speak with his mother first thing as soon as he got home from school today.

The final bell ending the school day rang at 3:00 p.m. sharp, which resulted in a mass stampede of kids wanting to get home. Daniel was no exception. He ran as fast as he could to get home. He wanted to interrogate his mother to find out more about the Pirates game and to probe her to see if there was a chance his family would purchase the tickets. He found his mother in the kitchen when he got home. She was wearing an apron and standing near the stove, attending to a large pot. He didn't know what she was cooking, but it smelled great. "Mom, what do you know about the Pirates doubleheader on July 17th?" he asked. Before she could respond, Daniel told her everything he had learned about the game in school today.

"Settle down, son," she responded. "We still have a lot of time to talk about this before we need to make a decision."

Daniel was impatient with her response. "Have you spoken to Dad about going?"

"No, Daniel, I haven't spoken to your father yet about any of this." Truth be told, Pauline hadn't even spoken to him about her volunteering for the Polish Festival Committee.

"Daniel, I need to tell you something, and you need to keep it a secret. I haven't told anyone, including your father and brothers." It was unlike his mother to confide in anything with him, let alone revealing a secret.

"What's the secret, Mom? he asked sheepishly.

"Daniel when I first volunteered on the Polish Festival Committee, I also agreed to open our home to any family attending the festival from out of town, so they would have a place to stay, free of charge. There is a family from a small town who live about sixty miles from Pittsburgh who responded and who will be staying with us during the Polish Festival Week. They are a family of five, who have three boys, one about your age. The problem is that I haven't told your father yet, and I'm not sure how he's going to accept the news."

Daniel stood there, shocked at first, not knowing what to say. He was unsure how he would like to have complete strangers in his home. "Where are these people from and what are their names?" Daniel asked. "They are from a Polish Parish in a small town called Windber, and their name is Brodziak. Kathryn and Ben are the parents, and they have three boys—Adam, Gregory, and Joseph. Adam is the oldest and is your age. They will be staying with us for the entire week, and guess what? Their dad plans to purchase tickets to the Pirates doubleheader."

Daniel's interest in these strangers immediately changed to being much more receptive to his mother's plans. "Does that mean we can get tickets too?" Daniel hopefully asked. "We'll see. I need to speak to your father first, so please keep what I told you a secret."

Daniel immediately sensed his mother's apprehension. Even if his dad agreed, it would unlikely that he could stay sober for a week. Hosting a family of five would be a daunting task and could serve to be a huge sort of embarrassment for his family if his father couldn't stop drinking for a week. That would be his mother's problem to deal with, but for now, Daniel looked upon this as being heaven sent. It would be impolite not to attend the game with their guests. He could only look now at his mother and prayed she would find the strength and courage to get his father to agree.

Chapter 20

The Swim Lesson

"Be careful today, Adam," his mother called as he left the kitchen of his home. He was on his way to swimming classes his mother had signed him up for at the Windber recreation park. School was over for the summer, and today was the first day of swimming lessons. He kissed his mother goodbye, grabbed his backpack, and began the long walk to the park. His parents had only one car, so Adam was told he would have the walk the two miles to where the swim classes were being held. Last summer, he and his brothers had walked to the park and discovered a shortcut, which he planned to use today. The journey would not be an easy one.

After leaving home, Adam walked the back alleys that lead from his home to Cambria Avenue. He followed Cambria Avenue until it dead-ended near the intersection of Nineteenth Street. It was here that he followed a dirt path down a steep ravine that took him to the foot of Paint Creek, which bordered Mine 42, one of ten smaller coal-mining patch communities that surrounded the small town of Windber.

Coal-mining had been the main source of employment for Windber since it was founded back in 1897 by the Berwind-White Coal Company when the company opened Eureka coal mine number 30 in 1897, followed by numbers 31 and 32. Eureka mine numbers 33, 34, 35, 36, 37, 38, 39, 40, 41, and 42 were opened shortly afterward. The town of Windber served at the regional headquarters of the Berwind-White Windber coalmining operations. The smaller patch towns surrounding Windber provided many of the coal miners with company-owned housing for the miners who worked in the mines. These homes were duplex-style homes designed to house two families in one building.

Although these houses provided a cramped living space for the mining families, they were located close to the entrances to the mines and enabled mines to walk a short distance from their home to work.

The town of Windber was the central point of the area's economy and provided religious, social, shopping, entertainment, and banking services for the residents and the surrounding coal-mining communities. Berwind-White sold lots to individuals who weren't necessarily coal miners. Some of these people were doctors, lawyers, and storekeepers. Many of them lived in these well-maintained homes. Beautiful churches, homes, banks, and hotels were built along tree-lined streets of Windber. The Eureka Store provided residents with a department store type of shopping where one could go to purchase anything from food to clothing to hardware supplies. The Arcadia Movie Theatre was located in the center of town along Graham Avenue, the main street of the town, and was the main source of entertainment for the community. The executives and community managers had constructed Victorian-style homes and mansions in the residential section of town. These homes were built in the hills overlooking the town, which provided their owners with a spectacular view of the valley below the town.

Over the years, the Berwind-White coal company began closing their operations in the Windber area, so by 1960, few mines remained operational. Mine 42 was one of the mines that were still operating and was the mine that Adam's father still worked. Both his grandfathers and all seven of his uncles all worked in the mines until they either retired or passed away. His grandfather came to Windber in 1909 from Poland and immediately began working in the mines. He bought a small farm on the outskirts of town and would purchase more surrounding land each year until he owned one of the largest farms in the Windber area.

When he was younger, his dad would work on the farm and coal mine at the same time. After World War II broke out, Adam's grandfather was unable to maintain the farm, so he sold it and moved to a smaller home closer to town. It was right before the war that Mine 42 suffered a collapse, which killed three miners. His father was working that day and suffered a broken leg, trying to save other miners to escape the disaster. He was never fully able to recover and, to this day, walks with a severe limp.

As Adam stood at the foot of Paint Creek, he looked up and could see the small twin homes that made up the Mine 42 community. The old coal tipple stood near the foot of the entrance to the mine and made Adam wonder what his dad was doing right now in the mine. He always prayed that his father would come home safely, but being a coal miner, one would never know what to expect.

Adam had to cross over the creek in order to rejoin the path on the other side. Crossing over the creek was the most dangerous part of his journey. Although the creek water ran swiftly by him, it was not very deep at this point and only about fifty feet wide. There were plenty of rocks protruding from the bed of the creek, which formed a natural bridge for him to cross over. Adam stepped cautiously over one rock at a time, making every effort to maintain his balance, not to fall. He let his momentum carry him from one rock to the next until he was safely on the other side of the creek. He stopped and looked behind him at the flowing waters and gave a sigh of relief that he had made it.

Ahead of him was the most difficult part of this hike. He followed the path up the embankment which put him in the middle of Mine 42 village. Railroad Avenue ran through the middle of Mine 42, which led from the village to the center of Winder below. Large dump trucks carrying coal used this route to carry coal from the mine and was always very busy with traffic. So Adam looked both ways before crossing. The path he had followed turned into a small side alley, which led to the foot of the steep forest-covered hill that he had to climb to get to the Windber recreational park and his swimming lesson class.

He passed a small grocery store that served not only to provide food but which contained a pool table were residences would go to shoot pool. The path he was following led behind the grocery store and to the foot of the hill that he would have to climb. Adam looked up and began to wonder if there was an easier way. Undaunted, Adam continued to follow the path up the hill. The path narrowed as Adam climbed higher and higher toward his ultimate destination. Branches from small trees and shrubs began to impede his way, and the path became rocky and slippery. Adam stopped and took a rest in an area where he felt was about half the way to the top. Here he turned around to better assess his position. Below him, he could see the town of Windber, picturesquely snuggled in the valley, surrounded by the beautiful rolling hills of Pennsylvania. He loved this view and felt reluctant to move forward, but his legs began to ache, so he turned and started to move up the hill.

The top of the hill began to gradually level off, and Adam knew that he was getting closer to the top. Suddenly, the path opened to a grass-covered field, then opened completely to the entrance of the Windber Recreational Park. Adam could see the swimming pool in the distance and could hear the shouts of other kids, who were getting ready for their swimming lesson.

His mother had packed his backpack with his swimming trunks, a towel, and a lunch of bologna and cheese sandwiches. Adam was unsure of what he had to do next, since this was his first swim lesson, so he walked to the front entrance of the gated pool, where he found someone wearing a lifeguard swimsuit. "Are you here to take swim lessons," the lifeguard asked.

What else would a young kid be doing at a pool this early in the morning? Adam thought but nodded his head in response.

"Okay, you can go into the men's locker room and change into your swimsuit," the guard instructed. "Then meet me over at the three-foot end of the pool."

Early June mornings were still cold in Western Pennsylvania, and this morning felt even more so, standing near a pool, wearing nothing but a pair of swim trunks. Adam wasn't looking forward to jumping into the cold three-foot end of the pool. He joined another

113

group who were standing near the pool, all shivering as he was. He didn't recognize any of these kids. He attended Parochial school at St. John Cantius, so he rarely had a chance to make friends with any of the kids who attended public school.

As Adam stood there, waiting for the swimming lessons to start, he was reminded about what his mother had told him early in the week. In response to the invitation she received in the mail, her parents had decided to accept the offer and would be traveling to Pittsburgh, Pennsylvania, to attend a Polish Festival in July. Their family would be taking a bus sponsored by their Parish to Pittsburgh, sometime in the middle of July. He initially felt excited about going, but now the prospect of living with another family for a week made him anxious. His mother had spoken to the lady who had sent the invitation and learned that they were a family of three boys, one of them was his age. His father had also purchased tickets to a Pirates doubleheader, so for the first time, he would be going to not one but two baseball games. He knew that his dad loved baseball, and the Pittsburgh Pirates were his favorite team. Adam did not share his enthusiasm for the sport, however, and was indifferent about going to see these games. Meeting someone new in a strange city and strange home also was not appealing.

His daydreaming ended with the abrupt whistle blown by the lifeguard who had greeted him at the front gate to the pool. It looked like this guy was in charge. "Okay, everyone, listen up," the lifeguard yelled. "My name is Mike, and for the next six weeks, I will be your swimming instructor. In order to pass your swimming lessons, you all will eventually have to be able to dive into the twelve-foot end of the pool and swim to length of the pool, but for now, we're starting you out in the three-foot end."

Everyone looked quietly at Mike and said nothing to their instructor.

"The first thing we're going to do today," said Mike, "is to learn to doggy paddle. Have any one of you seen a dog swim?" Without waiting for a response, Mike instructed, "A dog uses his front legs to paddle while keeping his head above water. That's what I want you to do today. Okay, everyone, in the pool."

One by one, the group entered the pool, some more bravely than others. When the cold water hit him, Adam felt like he was going to die. He quickly shook and splashed the water around him. Slowly his body became accustomed to the cold water, but he still could not stop shivering. Mike stood in front of the group in the water and demonstrated the doggy paddle technique of swimming. "Okay, I want you all to try," Mike invited.

It looked simple enough, but Adam felt awkward in his attempts to keep his head above water. With some determination, he was able to swim to the other side of the pool without stopping. "Excellent!" Mike yelled to Adam. "Way to go! What's your name?"

"I'm Adam," he responded.

"Okay, Adam, now swim back to the other end where you started."

Adam's confidence had improved as he plodded his way through the shallow end of the pool to the other side, where he stopped and stood up. He felt safe in the three-foot part of the pool since he was able to touch the bottom and stand up at any time, if he felt the need to do so. It won't be as easy in the deeper end of the pool, but Adam didn't want to think of that just yet.

After the students had all successfully traversed the length of the pool, Mike gathered them together. "Good job, everyone, on your first swim lesson. The idea eventually will be for you to learn to swim using strokes and breathing techniques that will require you to hold your breath as you dip your head underwater. For now, the doggy paddle stroke will do. We'll see you next week at the same time. Does everyone have a ride home?"

Adam looked around in response to this question. Was he the only one who had walked two miles to get to the class? Without saying a word, Adam went into the locker room, dried himself with the towel his mother had packed, got dressed, and walked quietly through the gate, where he had first come in.

Mike was waiting as his students began to leave. and stopped Adam before he could leave. "Hey, kid, do you have a ride home?" Mike asked.

"No, I walked here today, and I'm going to walk back home."

Mike looked around. "How far did you walk?" Mike asked.

"It's only about a two-mile walk," Adam replied. "No big deal."

Mike looked at him incredulously. This kid could be no more than eight years old. Walking that far was a big deal. "Listen, if you can wait a couple of minutes, I can give you a ride home. I do have to stop by the library first, but that should only take a few minutes."

Reluctantly, Adam agreed to accept his offer for a ride. He wasn't too sure if his mother would be crazy about him taking rides from a complete stranger. But his guy was a lifeguard, so Adam felt a degree of comfort in going with him. Besides, Adam had planned to visit the library sometime this week to see if the new *Black Stallion* book he had placed on reserve had yet to be returned to the library. This was a good opportunity for him to check in with the librarian.

Adam had discovered the book written by Walter Farley called *The Black Stallion* last summer, when he had to read three books during his summer break from school. It was a book about a kid named Alec Ramsey who was saved from a sinking ship while on his way from visiting his missionary uncle in India. Alec's uncle had booked him a ride home on a steamer that was scheduled to sail from India to New York City. En route, the steamer stopped at an Arabian port, where the captain of the ship reluctantly agreed to accept a wild black stallion as part of his freight. Shortly after departure, the ship encountered a severe storm somewhere near the Azur Islands, which caused it to sink after being struck by lightning. Alec was thrown free from the ship and was able to save himself when the black stallion swam next to him in the water. Alec was able to grab a rope that was attached to the stallion's halter and dragged it to the safety of a deserted island. The horse and Alec survived until they were eventually saved by a Portuguese fishing boat.

After returning to New York, Alec befriends retired racehorse trainer Henry Dailey, who lives near Alec in Flushing, New York. Henry trains the black stallion to race, and the book ends with the black stallion winning a well-publicized match race.

Adam loved the story so well that he read it three times that summer. He later discovered that Farley had written several other books, which were sequels to *The Black Stallion*. So now Adam wanted to read the follow-up book called *The Black Stallion Returns*. To his delight, he discovered that the library had acquired this book, and Adam made sure to reserve the book once it was back in stock.

Adam followed Mike to the parking lot where he got into his car. He looked around cautiously before he asked, "How long have you been driving?"

Mike looked at him and smiled. "Don't worry, I just got my driver's license last month. This is my dad's car. He lets me drive to swim class and back."

Adam looked in the back seat and saw lying there a blue and white jacket with a big white W sewed on the front. Adam recognized it as a Windber Ramblers letterman jacket. His dad had one he got after playing football for Windber High. "Do you play football? Adam asked.

Mike again smiled, this time without looking at Adam. "Yeah, do you believe I play quarterback for the Ramblers. I'm going into my senior year."

Adam was impressed. His father always boasted about the Windber Ramblers football team. His father played on two back-to-back undefeated seasons. Although Windber was a small town, they had a reputation for playing other high schools from much larger cities like Altoona, Erie, Steelton, and archrival Johnstown High School. "Wow, you must be pretty good," Adam replied, knowing that being the team's quarterback was a really big deal.

"We'll see. This will be the first time that I will be starting for the team," Mike humbly responded. "How about you. You're a pretty good swimmer. Do you play any sports?"

Adam looked down at his hands before responding. His dad had taken him to sign up for Little League baseball, but he quit before he even started. "No," Adam said. "I'm not much for sports. I am going to Pittsburgh in July to see the Pirates play," Adam said, trying to change the subject.

"Wow, that should be fun. They're playing really well. Did you know that the Pirates are in first place?"

Adam nodded his head, even though he didn't really know nor even cared.

After leaving the parking lot, Mike drove down Ninth Street before making a left onto Park Avenue. Park Avenue was a tree-lined residential area with beautifully landscaped single homes. Many of Windber's lawyers, doctors, and businessmen lived in this section of town. There weren't many coal-miners living in these homes. Mike turned right on Twelfth Street and stopped at the corner of Twelfth and Somerset Avenue. The library was located in the basement of the West End Elementary School located at this intersection. Mike parked his car and applied the emergency brake. Mostly, part of this section on Windber was located on steep hills, so having a good emergency brake was essential.

"Okay, I'll be right back," Mike said, "I just need to get a book."

"I need to go get a book myself," Adam advised. "Let's go then, kid, I still got to get you home."

Adam loved the smell of a library. The newer and older books blended to form an amora that made him feel comfortable. Adam walked up to the counter where the librarian was seated. "Can I help you young man," the librarian greeted.

"I'm here to pick up a book that I have on reserve."

"Okay, what's the name of the book?"

"I'm looking for a book by Walter Farley called *The Black Stallion Returns*," Adam responded.

The librarian left her station and walked to a cart containing a number of books. After searching through the cart, Adam saw her pull a book and return to the counter. "Here you go," she said. "Is this the book you're looking for?"

Adam grabbed the book, excited about the prospect of reading a new book about the Black Stallion. "Yes," Adam replied and began walking away.

"I need your library card before you can leave with the book."

Adam stopped short, suddenly realizing that he didn't have his card. He had not planned to go to the library today, so he hadn't brought it with him. "I don't have my library card," he told the librarian.

"Sorry, but I can't let you take it home without a library card. You can stay here and read the book." That wouldn't be possible since he knew that Mike wanted to get home and would not have time to wait. "What's the problem?"

Adam looked up and saw Mike standing behind him.

"He doesn't have his library card, Mike." It was obvious that she knew Mike by the way she spoke to him.

"Can I check it out on my library card, Ma. Simpson?"

"Sure, you can, Mike. I'll trust you."

Adam looked as Mike passed over his library card. "Make sure you return this book on time, kid, or it'll be my head." He smiled as he looked at Ms. Simpson, who was smiling back at him.

"Enjoy your book, son. It looks like a fun book."

Adam grabbed the book and walked out of the library with Mike at his side. "Gee, thanks, Mike. I'll make sure that I return it on time."

"I know you will. Let's get going, I need to take you home. My dad's going to wonder where I am."

Adam sat there, looking at his newly acquired book. The two of them said nothing more after driving away from the library until they got to Adam's house. "See you next week for swimming lessons. I hope you like your new book and have fun in Pittsburgh this summer."

Adam got out of the car and waved goodbye to his new friend. The summer of 1960 had just begun. It would soon become one that Adam would never forget.

Chapter 21

Final Preparations

Pauline scurried out of the front door to her home. Her husband was working the late shift tonight, so she had to wait until he was gone, before heading off to tonight's Polish Festival committee meeting. The festival was only two weeks away, and there was still plenty of work to be done. The committee had become a central point in her life as it was a much-needed distraction from her mundane home life and troubled marriage. She had eventually summoned the courage to let her husband know that she had volunteered to allow another family to share their home during Polish Festival week. To her surprise, Peter did not oppose the idea but in fact seemed to embrace it.

"It would be nice to meet other people," Peter said after being told. "It would also be good for the kids to make new friends with someone outside of Polish Hill."

Pauline had taken his response with some trepidation. It wasn't like her husband to be so understanding and accommodating. Since he had started drinking, he was a changed man from the one she married, one that made him very difficult to live with. Pauline still loved her husband but was feeling as though she was at the end of her rope with him. She knew that her Catholic faith demanded of her to endure and sacrifice and to do everything she could to save her marriage, short of leaving him.

"Peter, you need to promise me one important thing," she asked of her husband. "These people will be strangers in our house, and you need to stop drinking so long as they will be staying with us. I won't have this family being embarrassed. Do you understand me, Peter Pryzinski?" she demanded.

Peter looked at her with sober eyes before responding. It was rare that they ever had a decent conversation whenever he wasn't drinking. "Pauline, I don't have a drinking problem," Peter insisted. He always told her that whenever she confronted him. "So don't worry about me, you'll see. I'll make sure not to have anything to drink so you and the kids will be very proud of me."

Pauline looked at her husband and could only pray. This wasn't the first time he promised not to drink. His promises never lasted long. *It'll only be a week. So maybe he can go that far without drinking.* She could only hope.

Pauline walked into the church basement, just as George Zanecky was calling the meeting to order. He greeted her and allowed enough time for her to find a seat. "We're two weeks away now, folks. Are you guys getting excited?"

George was always so upbeat and enthusiastic about everything, which made him a good leader and advocate for whatever project he took over. There were about twenty members of the committee in attendance at tonight's meeting. Few responded with the same enthusiasm as George. It had been a long couple of months, and the committee had spent countless hours in preparation, so most were anxious for the Polish Festival to be over with.

The committee had been broken up into four groups. Pauline had volunteered for the decorating committee. The church Hall would serve to be the central point of the festival. The basement had been renovated years ago and now served as a gathering place for the church, where wedding receptions, school plays, bingo, and meetings were held on a regular basis. The church had also installed a state-of-the-art kitchen which rivaled any found in any one of Pittsburgh's high-end restaurants. The parishioners of Immaculate Heart of Mary Church took great pride in their banquet hall, which would now serve to host the many expected attendees to this year's festival.

Pauline's committee would be responsible for decorating the hall. This year, the festival would be held in honor of Our Lady of Czestochowa. Our Lady was a Polish icon, also lovingly known at the "Black Madonna" in Poland. The icon depicts a black-skinned Blessed Virgin Mary standing with the child Jesus in her arms. The miraculous icon became famous for its countless miracles. Over the centuries, these miracles have caused many pilgrims throughout Poland and from distant coasts of Europe to visit the Marian Shrine of Jasna Gora. The chapel that housed the painting came under attack in the 1600s and was set on fire, causing its complete destruction.

Legend has it that the painting survived the fire but caused the face of the Virgin and Child Jesus to turn black. Pauline had the responsibility of securing a copy of the Our Lady of Czestochowa painting so it could be displayed in the church hall for the duration of the Polish Festival. Through much effort, Pauline was able to locate and borrow the icon from the National Shrine of Our Lady of Czestochowa in Doylestown, Pennsylvania, a small city located fifty miles from Philadelphia. In addition, her committee was responsible for purchasing flowers and streamers in the traditional red-and-white colors of Poland. Polish flags of all sizes were also purchased to fly both inside and outside of the church's property.

An area consisting of six square blocks surrounding the church would be blocked off to all but pedestrian traffic. Other committees were placed in charge of securing entertainment, which included some of the best Polka Bands in the tri-county area and Polish dancers dressed in traditional Polish costumes. The plan was to have these bands playing day and night for the entertainment of the festival goers. Amusement rides would be set up on the church parking lot. Some of the rides would include a Ferris wheel, bumper cars, a haunted house, a roller coaster, and a fun house among others. Carnival games like High Striker, Milk Bottle Knockdown, Ring Toss, Bust-a-Balloon, Basketball Free Throw, and Skeet-Ball would also be available to provide patrons with the opportunity to win various prizes or tickets for redemption for food or rides. Food trucks were also invited to the festival to sell their various food items directly from their trucks. Contracts had to be negotiated with all of these vendors. The proceeds of the Polish Festival would benefit the Immaculate Heart of Mary Church and the school.

A raffle ticket committee was also established to sell raffle tickets for a chance to win a brand-new car. A local Cadillac car dealership had donated a 1960 DeVille coupe. The car would be raffled off on Saturday night, July 16, which the committee had hoped to be the most well-attended night of the festival. The car would be displayed in front to the church the entire week. The committee was hoping to raise over $100,000 from the sale of these car raffle tickets.

George Zanecky personally chaired the Pirates Day committee. George was successful in purchasing a block of two hundred tickets from the Pirates for the July 17 doubleheader with the Cincinnati Reds. The seats were located directly behind the Pirates' dugout and would provide the ticketholders with an excellent view of Forbes Field. The Pirates also agreed to honor the Immaculate Heart of Mary Church and the Polish Festival during the game.

George had represented the Pirates in various negotiations with the City of Pittsburgh, which helped him to purchase the tickets from the Pirates for half price. These tickets would be sold at full price to anyone interested in attending the game on a first come, first serve basis.

George began the meeting with brief prayer to St. Joseph, then he called upon each committee chairman to provide the group with their individual reports. Pauline was the first to be called upon. Her report was brief, at which time she advised what decorations would be provided and at what cost. After providing her report, Pauline sat back in her chair and listened as the rest of the chairpersons provided their updates.

George was the last to give his report. "First of all, I want everyone to know that thanks to the generosity of many of our parishioners, we will be able to provide free housing to over two hundred families who will be attending the festival from out of town. I know that this was no easy endeavor, and the hospitality of those willing to share their homes is greatly appreciated. I also want you to know that I have also been able to sell all two hundred tickets to the July 17th Pirates game."

Everyone stood and applauded George for his efforts. Pauline, however, was dismayed at hearing this news. She had meant to speak to her husband about buying tickets to the Sunday doubleheader but hadn't. She never expected them to sell so quickly. It would have been a good time for Peter to take their sons to a game. He very seldom did anything with them. She didn't know what she was going to tell the boys, especially Daniel, who had his heart on going to see a doubleheader. He so loved the Pirates. Pauline decided to wait until the last minute before breaking the news to him.

After George completed his report, he turned the meeting over to Father Damian, who had joined the meeting late. Father thanked everyone who had volunteered and expressed his appreciation on behalf of his Parish. It was hoped that the festival would help raise a million dollars. Given what he had heard, Father felt confident that the parish would reach their goal.

"Father, can you give us your blessing to help close out tonight's meeting?" George asked from his place at the podium.

Without saying a word, Father Damian turned to group and made the sign of the cross while saying, "I bless you in the name of the Father, the Son, and the Holy Ghost."

Pauline accepted the blessing, crossed herself, and grabbed her purse. She was ready to exit the door when she heard George call her name. "Pauline, can you wait a second?" he asked.

The meeting had gone later than she had expected, so she was anxious to get back home to check on the boys and was annoyed at having to wait. George grabbed her arm as both walked out into the darkness outside. He turned and looked at Pauline before placing his hand into one of his pants pockets. Pauline watched as George retrieved an envelope and handed it to her. "Here," he said. "I won't be able to use these."

Pauline opened the envelope which, to her surprise, contained five tickets to the Pirates doubleheader on July 17. "I don't have the money to pay for these tickets, George." She tried to return them to him.

"Don't worry about it, Pauline. I don't have any kids or anyone else I can take to the game. So they're yours at no charge. Let's say it's my way of thanking you for all your help with this year's committee."

Pauline looked at him, a little confused. As far as she was concerned, her efforts were minor in comparison with the others on the committee. "This is very generous of you, George. I don't know what to say, but thanks. My boys are going to be very happy when I tell them," she said, not knowing what else to say.

"Maybe your husband would like to go as well," George said. Pauline just looked at him and nodded. "Can I give you a ride?" George asked, trying to change the subject.

"No, that's okay. I need the walk. It's such a lovely night."

George looked up at the star-filled night sky and, without say a word, got into his car. As he drove away, Pauline began to wonder what life would have been like if she had married George instead of her husband. She shook her head, trying to relieve herself of that thought and began walking home.

Chapter 22

Home Away from Home

Adam stood on the front step of the bus where he was able to see inside. He had never been on a bus before and was unsure what to expect. "Move inside, Adam. Go to the back of the bus," his father prompted. He was standing right behind him along with his mother and two brothers. Their long-anticipated trip to Pittsburgh was about to begin. The family had gotten up early to catch the bus that was waiting for them in the parking lot of St. John Cantius church. His family was one of fifty-six parishioners who had booked the bus trip to attend the Polish Festival in Pittsburgh. This would also be the first time that Adam had ever left his hometown. He was still very apprehensive, especially having to stay with a strange family in their home for an entire week. His parents had tried to sell the idea as some kind of "big adventure" that all would enjoy.

Adam wasn't buying it, however, and now wished he could stay at home. In response to his father's demands, Adam moved toward the back of the bus, where several other passengers had already grabbed their seats. The bus appeared new with plenty of room and comfortable-looking seats. Adam found a seat and removed the backpack he was carrying and placed it at the foot of the seat as he sat down. Adam had selected a window seat, which he wanted so he could have a better view during their trip. Pittsburgh was only a two-hour bus ride from Windber, but to a kid who never went anywhere, it seemed like it would be a long trip. Adam reached down and retrieved a book he had stored in his backpack. He had insisted that he be allowed to take a book to read to help pass the time until they got to Pittsburgh. His dad sat next to him, while his mother and two brothers took two other seats across the aisle from them.

"Do you really think that you'll have time to read that book, Adam?" his father asked as both became more comfortable in their seats. He was glad that he was sitting next to his father on this trip instead of sitting next to his brothers. Both were younger than him, and he knew both would be a handful for his parents during this trip. His Uncle Frank had wanted to join them but decided at the last minute to pass on the going. Adam wished that his parents would let him stay home with his uncle but knew better than asking them if he could.

"Good morning, Doctor," he heard his mother call out. "Glad you and your wife can make the trip."

Adam looked up to see Dr. Tom Slevic and his wife, Ann, take the seats directly in front of his mother. Dr. Tom, as the family called him, was their family doctor who made many house calls over the years to attend to their family, especially the boys, who were always coming down with some sort of childhood sickness. Last summer, he had stepped on a rusty nail, which became infected. Dr. Tom had diagnosed him as having "blood poisoning," for which he treated Adam with antibiotics and Epsom salt wraps. Being a young kid, all kinds of crazy things had gone through Adam's mind after learning about his infection, including the possibility of him dying.

Dr. Tom was able to ease his mind, but to this day, Adam remains cautious about where he steps to avoid stepping on another rusty nail. The doctor also treated his brother Greg last winter after he developed pneumonia after the boys had spent a long day sledding down the farm field next to their home. Although Adam didn't know it at the time, his brother's condition had been far worse than his infected foot. He would learn years later that Greg had almost died from his condition. He still remembered seeing his father kneeling at the foot of Greg's bed, crying and praying. Fortunately, thanks to Dr. Tom's care, Greg recovered after being sick for over two months with pneumonia. The effects of this disease would eventually have a long-term effect on Greg's health, which caused him to be sickly most of his life. Because of this, Adam had an enduring affection for Dr. Tom and was glad to see that he was joining them for this trip to Pittsburgh.

"Hello, Kathryn, good to see you as well. I'm really looking forward to going to this festival. We should have a great time. Did you guys get tickets to the Pirates game?"

"We wouldn't miss seeing the Pirates play," his father responded to his wife. "I'm taking the boys to the game. It'll be our first time to Forbes Field, and we can't wait. Right, Adam?" his father said, turning his gaze to his oldest son.

Adam just looked up sheepishly and shrugged his shoulders. Even though he had no interest in going, Adam felt a sense of responsibility as the oldest son and didn't want to disappoint his father. "The Pirates are really playing well, aren't they?" said the doctor. "Seeing them play two games in one day is going to be great!"

Changing the subject, his father said, "Hey, Doc, I heard that you started working at the Somerset County alcohol rehab center in Somerset."

Dr. Tom looked at Ben and nodded. He didn't realize that anyone knew just yet, but word travels quickly in a small town. The center was located in the town of Somerset, Pennsylvania, only about a thirty-minute drive from Windber. "Yes, I've agreed to work as the center's medical director. For now, I'll be doing part-time on a volunteer basis. So many of my patients are in need of help, so I decided to do something about it."

His father gave the doctor an understanding glance. It was not easy being a coal miner, and many of Ben's friends and coworkers turned to alcohol to help get them through after working all day in the mines. It was kind of a joke in town. Windber had plenty of two things, churches and bars. After spending a Saturday night drinking, one could easily find a church to attend to the following Sunday. "Good for you, Doc," his father responded. "Wish you the best of luck."

Adam heard the door to the bus close and realized that they were about to depart on their journey. The bus was completely full, and even though it was early, everyone was talking and eager to get underway. As the bus pulled from the parking lot, a cheer went up from several passengers. Adam felt a sense of merriment that he knew would continue for the rest of the drive to Pittsburgh. The bus turned left onto Graham Avenue, the main street of Windber, and drove a mile to Twelfth Street, where the driver made a tight turn. Twelfth Street took the bus to the entrance to Route 56 bypass.

Pennsylvania Route 56 (PA 56) is a 108-mile-long (174 km) state highway located in west central Pennsylvania. Its western terminus is at the eastern end of the C. L. Schmitt Bridge in New Kensington. Its eastern terminus is on US Route 30 (US 30), west of Bedford. Before the bypass was constructed, Route 56 went right through the heart of Windber's downtown area. With the construction of the bypass, traffic was being diverted away from the center of Windber, making travel around the area easier. Adam looked out his window as the town grew smaller and smaller.

Route 56 took them west through the City of Johnstown, PA, which was a bustling city of about sixty thousand people. Johnstown was noted for his steel and iron works. Back in 1889, the city and its steel mills were completely destroyed after being flooded by waters following a dam burst, twenty miles north of the city. In addition to the complete destruction of its industries, 2,200 residents of Johnstown also lost their lives in the flood. Johnstown was located in a narrow valley surrounded by steep mountains where rainfall would dump into the Conemaugh River which ran through the middle of the city. The city's geography made it susceptible to flooding, so in response, the city built an incline plane on the side of the mountain that residents could use to escape any future floods.

The incline plane quickly became a landmark and a tourist attraction after it was completed. As the bus drove through Johnstown, it passed directly by the entrance to the inclined plane. Adam looked intently, wondering what it would be like to take the inclined plane up to the top of the mountain. His father told him that there was a small town at the top called Westmont, which overlooked the city. His father had promised to take the family for a ride up the incline plane someday soon. Seeing it in person, Adam now couldn't wait. He was now hoping that their journey would take them past other cool places.

Route 56 took their bus north through Johnstown to the intersection of Route 22. As the bus made its turn onto Route 22, Adam saw the signs "Pittsburgh 60 miles west" and "Altoona 20 miles east." They still had a long way to go, but Adam was beginning to feel less apprehensive. *This trip may not be a bad idea after all*, he thought as the bus sped up onto Route 22.

Route 22 varied from a two-lane highway to a one-lane, depending on where you were driving at the time. After making its turn to go west toward Pittsburgh, the landscape turned to almost all rural, with rolling hills and acres of dairy farmland in all directions. Blairsville, Pennsylvania, was the first major town they came to on their way and marked the halfway point to Pittsburgh. For some reason, Route 22 changed to Route 119 as one drove through Blairsville and changed back to Route 22 once one reached New Alexandria, Pennsylvania.

Adam had settled into his seat and was comfortable watching as they made their way through this part of Pennsylvania he had never seen before. His father was right. He had lost all interest in reading his book and enjoyed instead quietly taking in the sights. He had lost a sense of time, so when he looked at his watch, he was surprised to see that it was already 10:00 a.m. His father had assured him that they would be in Pittsburgh soon. Near Export, Pennsylvania, Adam began to notice more and more homes and less farms. By the time they got to Murrysville, Adam could tell that they were close to their destination. The bus passed by the Monroeville Mall before turning onto Route 376, which would take them to downtown Pittsburgh. The volume of traffic increased the closer they got and at times came to a complete stop. This was what it was like living near a big city. Ahead, Adam could see what looked like a tunnel, and he asked his dad, "Do we have to go through a tunnel?"

"Yes, son, we have to go through the Squirrel Hill Tunnel."

The City of Pittsburgh was surrounded by mountains, so tunnels had been built to help facilitate the flow of traffic around and through the city. Adam had never been through a tunnel before, so he didn't know what to expect. The bus suddenly went dark as it entered the tunnel. There were lights inside of the tunnel, but still it felt like nighttime inside the bus. Adam looked outside in amazement, wondering how long it took to construct this tunnel. Before he knew it, the bus had made its way through and was on the other side. Beautiful homes lined the highway at this point, and Adam could see a large bridge overhead. A road sign announced an exit for Schenley Park and the University of Pittsburgh. The bus passed this exit and continued its way forward to Downtown Pittsburgh.

Adam could now see the large building that made up the business district of the city. As it neared downtown Pittsburgh, the bus turned off of Route 376 onto Route 579 north, then connected with Route 380. Adam looked around at the large skyscrapers that surrounded the bus as it drove forward. At some point, Route 380 turned into Bigelow Boulevard. From there, the bus made a left turn onto Herron Avenue, then a quick left onto Phelan Way. The bus pulled in front of a large Catholic church where the driver stopped and parked. Adam could see a sign in front announcing that they were parked in front of the Immaculate Heart of Mary Church.

"Looks like we've made it," his father announced. "That wasn't a bad ride, was it, Adam?"

Adam was too busy taking in the sights to respond to this father. He would soon learn that the Immaculate Heart of Mary Church was the central location of the Polish Festival and that they were to gather first in the church hall where they would meet their host family.

The passengers on the bus began to get up to leave, many of them stretching and groaning after their long drive. One by one, everyone, including Adam's family, got off the bus. As he stepped onto the sidewalk where the bus was parked, Adam looked around and was amazed to see how close the surrounding homes were to one another and to the church. The rowhouses that lined the streets were well maintained and brightly decorated, with flowers and Polish flags in celebration of the upcoming Polish festival.

Adam wondered how people could live so close to one another but then realized that this was the way city folks lived. Then he thought about which one of these homes his family would be living in for the next week. There possibility couldn't be enough room for two families to live in.

Adam's father had assembled the family outside the bus and was waiting to retrieve their luggage, which was stored in compartments underneath the bus. His mother had packed two large suitcases she borrowed from a neighbor, and as the bus driver pulled them to the curb, she began to wonder if she had packed enough clothes to last a week. After getting their luggage, Adam's father pulled a letter from one of his pockets and began to read it. The letter contained instructions about where they were to meet with their host family. They were staying with the Pryzinski family who lived at 34 Paulowna Street, which the letter said was only a few blocks from the church.

The letter instructed them to gather in the church hall and to wait there for the Pryzinskis to meet them. From there, they would walk to their home. So, after rereading the letter, Adam's father grabbed one of the suitcases and started walking up the stairs of the church with his family following closely behind. His wife was struggling with the other piece of luggage but managed to keep up. Before going too far up the steps, a sign greeted them. "Welcoming Center," it read with an arrow pointing in the direction they were to follow. This led them to the front door of the church hall, which was actually the basement of the church.

The hall was busy with activity as they entered and looked around. Long tables had been set up with the names of various host families written on signs and in alphabetical order. Looking for the P section, Adam's father was able to locate the sign for the Pryzinski family. To his dismay, no one was there to greet them. "Looks like we're going to have to wait," Ben said, sounding a little disappointed. He was so looking forward to meeting these people. Shortly afterward, an attractive young woman came running up to them, out of breath.

"Sorry I'm late, folks. My name is Pauline Pryzinski. You'll be staying with me and my family," she said as she shook Ben's hand. "And you must be Kathryn. I was so looking forward to meeting you. These must be your boys. Hi, kids, my boys are really looking forward to meeting you, so why don't we get going? It's only a short walk."

Everything was happening so fast that his parents could hardly say a word. Adam's mom and dad exchanged glances as they followed Pauline out the door with luggage in hand. "This way," Pauline directed as they exited the church hall. "I'm so glad that you've decided to come to Pittsburgh to celebrate the Polish Festival with us this year. We're going to have a great time."

Adam sensed a little anxiety in Pauline's voice, which made her sound a little uncertain about the upcoming events.

The house on 34 Paulowna Street was a four-story stand-alone building located on a plot of land with beautiful scrubs on one side and a small garden on the other. It was not the rowhouse that Adam had expected after seeing the other homes in the neighborhood. It was bigger than the other homes and was well maintained and decorated. Live plants hung from the ceiling of the front porch which overlooked Paulowna Street. A Polish and an American flag were predominantly displayed which gave a festive air to the home.

Adam felt a sense of relief as they walked up the concrete steps to the front door of the home. *This place doesn't look so bad*, he thought as Pauline gave the front door a knock before opening it to go in. "We're here!" she announced as she entered into the living room.

Sitting there was a man and three boys. "Welcome, welcome," the man said as they walked behind Pauline.

"This is my husband, Peter, and my three sons, Michael, Luke, and Daniel."

On cue, the boys stood up and, without saying a word, shook the hands of each member of the Brodziak family. "Sit down, sit down," Peter said in a very welcoming matter. "You folks must be very tired after your long bus ride."

Without waiting for a response Peter continued with his questioning, "You folks are from Windber, I understand. I've never been there. How long was the ride?"

"It took us about two hours to get here by bus, so we're not too far from Pittsburgh," Ben responded. "Windber's a small coal-mining town fifteen miles from Johnstown. I work in one of the coal mines that provides coal to the steel mills in both Johnstown and Pittsburgh," Ben proudly continued.

"I work for US Steel here in Pittsburgh, small world," Peter responded. Peter looked at his new friend with interest. *He's a fellow blue-collar union man. I already like this guy,* Peter thought. "Would you folks like some coffee? Pauline makes a great cup of coffee if I say so myself."

Pauline looked at her husband. That was the first time he'd ever complimented her for anything, let alone her coffee. "Yes, my apologies. You could probably use some coffee after your long ride. Boys, why don't you take the kids upstairs and show them to their rooms while I make coffee and get acquainted with the adults?"

The boys from both families looked at one another and didn't move. Finally, Mike spoke up and said, "Let's go upstairs. Your rooms are on the fourth floor."

Without saying a word, the Brodziak boys got up and followed their counterparts up a nearby set of stairs that led from the living room.

"Pauline, let me help you with the coffee. Let's give the men some time to get acquainted.," Kathryn offered as Pauline got up to go into the kitchen.

"That would be lovely," Pauline responded. "Follow me."

Kathryn looked around as she followed Pauline into the kitchen. The kitchen was small but well-kept, clean, and organized. A large pot was sitting on top of the gas stove, empty and showing the wear and tear of a long time from feeding a family of five. Pauline reached into a large cabinet and withdrew a jar labeled Coffee.

"How do you and Ben like your coffee?" Pauline asked as she laid the jar of coffee onto the countertop.

"We both like our coffee black, thank you," Kathryn responded as Pauline pulled the coffee pot from another cabinet under the sink.

"Great, that'll be easy."

Pauline poured several large scoops of coffee into the strainer of the coffee pot. *I hope I'm not making it too strong. She and her husband will be up all night,* Kathryn thought without saying a word to her hostess.

"Listen, Pauline, I really want to thank you and your husband for letting us stay at your place. We've been looking forward to this for some time now. It's hard to believe that we're finally here. Your husband is very charming."

Pauline looked at her guest and hesitated, wondering if she should confide in Kathryn about her husband's drinking problems. She decided not to say anything and responded by simply saying, "He has his moments." Peter had not had a drop to drink in over a week, so she wanted to leave well enough alone. Maybe her prayers had finally been answered, and her husband had stopped drinking for good.

She turned to her guest, saying, "The festival officially begins tomorrow, Saturday night at six. Several of our neighbors are also hosting families from out of town, so we are having a welcoming dinner for all the visiting families here at my house tomorrow night. There will be a dance at the church hall tomorrow night, just for the adults. The kids can go to the carnival that is right next door in the church parking lot. It should be a great time and will give us a better opportunity to get to know one another."

"That sounds wonderful," Kathryn responded. "I haven't been to a dance since my high school prom!"

Without either woman noticing, the coffee had stopped percolating and was ready to be served. The aroma from the freshly brewed coffee filled the air and smelled delicious as Pauline poured four cups. "Let's see how the men are doing," Pauline said as she picked up the tray where she had placed the cups of coffee. As the two returned to the living room, they heard their husbands laughing and talking about the Pirates and how well they were doing this season.

"I'm glad you and the boys are going to the doubleheader next Sunday. Forbes Field is such a great place to see a baseball game, and it looks like we have great seats. There is no better way to spend a Sunday afternoon but to watch a baseball game. Better still, two baseball games in one afternoon.," Peter said.

Pauline looked at the two men, thinking that they were both alike in many respects. *Maybe Peter needs a new friend that he could talk too without going to a bar.*

In the meantime, Adam and his two younger brothers had followed the Pryzinski boys up the narrow and steep steps that led to the first-floor landing. From there, they turned to another set of stairs that led to the upper two levels of the house. Finally, they got to the fourth floor, where Michael, the oldest boy, turned around and opened the first door he came to. "Here you go. We have four bedrooms up here, so you guys have your choice of rooms. I suggest that you let your parents stay in the one at the end of the hall. That one is bigger than these other bedrooms."

Adam looked into the room where he found a large, comfortable-looking bed with a dresser on one side and a small desk on the other. A ceiling fan hung from the ceiling, which was controlled by a switch on the wall. Adam entered the room and sat on the bed. Even though it was midsummer and hot outside, the room was surprisingly cool.

"Come on, you guys, get yourselves situated. I want to show you my room and my baseball card collection," Daniel, the youngest of the boys said. "I hope you like baseball. Come on, follow me," Daniel said without waiting for a response.

He must think everyone likes baseball, Adam thought as he followed young Daniel down the stairs to the third floor. His two younger brothers followed, too shy to venture on their own. Daniel opened the door to his bedroom. It looked like a baseball museum. "I don't usually let anyone in this room, especially my brothers, but my mother told me that I had to be nice to you guys being that you're our guests." Hanging on the walls of Daniel's bedroom were posters of baseball players, mostly members of the Pittsburgh Pirates, and baseball pennants containing the names of what appeared to be all of the Major League baseball teams. On his dresser, baseballs were displayed in plastic holding cases. As he got closer, Adam noticed that each ball contained an autograph, which he assumed was of some baseball player.

The boys stood there as Daniel dropped down to his knees at the foot of his bed and retrieved a cardboard box from underneath the bed. "These are my baseball cards that I've been collecting since I was a kid. Do you guys collect baseball cards?" Daniel asked. Without waiting for a response, he opened the box and dumped the contents on his bed.

There must be over three hundred cards, Adam thought. *Where did he get them all?*

Before he could continue, Mike Pryzinski burst into the bedroom.

"Get out of here, Mike! I'm going to tell Mom. You know I don't like you to come into my bedroom."

Mike looked at the boys and laughed. "Okay, Dan, I didn't want to get you mad, but Mom sent me up to get you boys. She wants to know if you want something to eat."

Daniel had been so preoccupied with his new living quarters that he had forgotten that it was well past afternoon and that they hadn't eaten since they left the bus.

Adam looked at his new friend, and although he had no interest in looking at baseball cards, he said, "I could use something to eat. We can look at your cards later on. After all, we'll be here all week."

Daniel looked at Adam, then back to his baseball cards. He quickly gathered them up and placed them back into the cardboard box and gently returned them to the hiding place underneath the bed. "Okay," Daniel said somewhat reluctantly. He had really looked forward to meeting this new family and showing off his baseball card collection.

As the boys exited the bedroom, Adam turned to look. *So this is going to be my home away from home for the next week,* he thought before closing the door to Daniel's bedroom. *This is a lot better than I thought it would be.*

Chapter 23

The Festival

Adam awoke from a deep sleep with a start. Staring down at him was a ceiling fan, twirling a cool breeze onto his face. Bright light from the early morning sunrise illuminated the unfamiliar room where he was lying in bed. It took several seconds for him to remember that he had spent his first night in his new bedroom at the Pryzinski home. Even though this was the first time he had ever spent away from home, in a strange bed, he had slept surprisingly well and felt refreshed after the long day his family had the day before. He could hear noises coming from the downstairs area of the home. The smell of breakfast filled the air, which made him realize that he hadn't eaten since yesterday and was hungry.

Looking down from his bed, Adam was able to find his pants lying on the floor next to the shirt he had worn the day before. He quickly got dressed, hoping that later on, his mom would provide him with a change of clothes. At this point, however, Adam did not care what he was wearing. He just wanted to find the rest of his family and get something to eat. He turned to look down the hall as he left his room. The door to the room where his parents were staying was open. He could see that they were no longer in the room. Open suitcases lay on the floor, showing evidence that his parents had tried to unpack before going downstairs. The doors to the bedrooms where his brothers were sleeping were closed, and he assumed that they were still asleep.

Adam crept quietly down the steps to the next floor. The floorboards creaked as he stepped down to the third-floor landing. As he began to turn the corner, the bedroom door next to him suddenly opened. Daniel Pryzinski stood there in his pajamas and, without saying a word, grabbed Adam's arm and pulled him inside and closed the door. The two boys stood there, looking at one another before Daniel broke the silence. "I was hoping it was you that was awake," Daniel said as he pulled Adam farther into his room. "I wanted to finish showing you my baseball card collection."

On the bed were hundreds of baseball cards covering every corner of the bed. Several cards had spilled over and were lying on the floor. "Where did you get all of these cards?" Adam asked, also wondering quietly how long it had taken the boy to collect them.

"Anytime I get an allowance, I usually go down to our local grocery store to buy a pack. They're only a nickel, and you normally get ten cards in a pack. I've been collecting them for as long as I can remember. I have baseball cards for almost every team in the Major League. I trade them with other guys who may have duplicates they don't need but that I don't have."

Adam grabbed a card to take a closer look. The card showed the photo of a guy named Rubén Amaro. The card identified him as a shortstop with a team called the Philadelphia Phillies. *A strange name for a baseball team*, thought Adam, not realizing that the nickname for the City of Philadelphia was Philly. "Turn the card over," Daniel instructed.

Turning the card over, Adam could see a series of numbers and years, all of which meant nothing to him. "These are the various seasons this player has played so far and his batting record for each year. This guy hasn't been playing for very long since the card only contained the stats for two years. The Phillies aren't a very good team this year, but they managed to split a doubleheader with the Pirates yesterday. See this," Daniel said, holding up a book for Adam to see. "I used this book to record the score of yesterday's games between the Pirates and the Phillies. Do you know how to keep a score of a baseball game? I can teach you if you don't."

Adam took the book and looked it over, again not knowing exactly what he was looking at. The book contained the names of various individual players, and next to them letters and numbers which made no sense to Adam. "You use this book to keep a record of each at bat for each player. These numbers are used to calculate the players' batting average. If a player gets a hit at every at bat, his average would be 1.00, which is impossible. Most major league baseball players have a batting average of around .250. The really good ones bat above .300, but the great ones hit over .350."

Although he was good at math, these numbers made Adam's head spin. He wasn't too sure if he really wanted to know how to keep score of a baseball game, but he would try as a courtesy to his new friend. "I can't wait to learn.," Adam said, more to appease his host.

"I'm getting hungry," Adam said to change the subject.

"Okay, but before we go downstairs, I want to show you one more thing.," Daniel said as he reached down and pulled another large box from underneath his bed. As he opened the box, Daniel said, "I don't show this to many people."

Adam's curiosity made him forget about food. Inside the box were three large albums. Daniel carefully pulled each album from the box and gently place each one on the bed. The first album he opened contained more baseball cards. This time, however, the cards were of players all wearing the Pittsburgh Pirates' baseball uniform. "I have collected the cards of each of the players for the Pirates over the past three years.," Daniel proclaimed proudly as he turned one page after another. The cards appeared to be an alphabetical order by the players' last names, and on many occasions, there were more than one of the same cards, duplicates as Daniel had called them. Daniel went from one album to the next before saying anything. "Every time I get the card for a Pittsburgh Pirate player, I place the card into one of these albums. I think I've collected them all, but I'm not certain."

Adam stood there, amazed, and wondered how much time and effort it had taken for his new friend to work on these albums. He looked at Daniel with newfound admiration. *This guy really loves baseball*, Adam thought, making him wonder what he was missing.

Maybe he should start to pay more attention to this game of baseball. "This is amazing, Daniel," Adam said. "Let's get something to eat. I'd love to learn more from you about baseball, so you can teach me later, if you don't mind."

Daniel looked at Adam and smiled. He'd love nothing more than to talk about baseball with anyone, especially someone of his own age. He closed his albums, returned them to their box and, along with the rest of his baseball card collection, placed them back underneath his bed. "Let's go. My mom makes a great breakfast." He grabbed Adam's arm, and both boys raced to the first-floor kitchen.

The two boys arrived at the kitchen together and were greeted by the rest of both families, who were already sitting in the kitchen eating their breakfast, including Adam's younger brothers, whom he thought were still asleep upstairs.

"Good morning, boys. Nice of you to join us this morning," Pauline Pryzinski said greeting them with a welcoming smile.

"I was showing Adam my baseball card collection," Daniel explained.

"I'm surprised that he let you come down at all from that bedroom. One of these days, I'm going to throw all those cards away," Daniel's mother teased.

Daniel gave his mother a disdainful glare, not appreciating her attempt at humor. Adam could feel Daniel's pain, having a greater understanding of what his collection meant to his new friend.

"We've been talking about our plans for this upcoming week at the Polish festival," Adam's mother chimed in. "We have a full week of activities planned for you boys. You're going to have a great time," she continued. "Sit down and have something to eat, and we'll fill you in on the details."

Both boys grabbed two unoccupied chairs and sat down at the table.

"What can I get you boys to eat? We have pancakes, scrambled eggs, waffles, bacon, and toast."

Before he could answer, Mrs. Pryzinski had placed a plate full of pancakes, scrambled eggs, and bacon in front of Adam. "Do you like maple syrup, Adam?" she continued.

"Yes please," Adam responded with delight. He loved pancakes and syrup. Adam glazed over to his partner whose plate contained only a stack of pancakes. Adam figured that Daniel's mother already knew what her son wanted for breakfast, which explained why he wasn't given the same options.

By the time they began to eat, the rest of the family had already dispersed throughout the house, leaving Adam and Daniel alone in the kitchen with their mothers. Adam's father and Mr. Pryzinski had made it to the porch at the front of the house, where they were sitting on two comfortable-looking rocking chairs. "The Pryzinskis are having a big dinner party tonight," Adam's mother said as she sat next to her son, watching him eat his breakfast. "They've invited two neighboring families to join us as part of a welcoming celebration. "Their neighbors are also hosting families from out of town this week. It'll be nice for us to meet other people. After dinner, the adults will all be going to a dance at the church hall, while you boys can have fun at the carnival which will be next door in the church parking lot. You boys need to promise me that you'll behave."

Several adults from the parish had volunteered as chaperones to watch the kids, so Adam's mother warned that she would know if anyone misbehaved. Adam was excited about going to the carnival. Every summer back home in Windber, the town would host a week-long carnival with all kinds of rides and amusements. If tonight's carnival was anything like the one back home, Adam was expecting to have a great time.

Just then, Mr. Pryzinski came walking back into the kitchen. "Ben and I are going to take the boys for a walk after breakfast. I thought I'd show them around the neighborhood." He walked over and gave his wife a kiss.

Pauline looked at her husband with some surprise and with a red face. It had been a long time since Peter had given her a kiss. "I thought we'd walk to Kaibur's for lunch," Peter continued.

That was our old hangout, Pauline reminisced. They would go there all the time when they first started dating, but they hadn't been there together in years. Pauline felt that it was strange that her husband wanted to go there now with people they just met. She silently wished she could go herself, but only with her husband. "Try not to get there too late," Pauline warned. "I don't want them to ruin their appetite for dinner. We're going to have plenty of food to eat tonight."

"I just want to get them some good Polish pastries," Peter said in response. This comment did not help to ease Pauline's mind.

It was ten-thirty by the time Adam and Daniel had finished their breakfast and got dressed. His brothers and the Pryzinski boys were already outside playing in the backyard. Only Michael Pryzinski was missing from the group. Daniel informed the rest that his oldest brother was working a paper route and normally didn't get home until after lunchtime. Adam walked into the backyard and was surprised to see how small it was.

"Not much room to play out here," Adam said more to himself but loud enough for Daniel Pryzinski to hear him.

"How much room do you need?" Daniel asked.

Before Adam could respond, Daniel led them to the side of the house, where a tall oak tree stood, providing the property with a welcome shade from the July sun. Adam loved to climb trees and felt comfortable when Daniel invited him to climb the tree with him. "We built a tree house up there, so follow me, and I'll show you," Daniel invited.

Hammered to the tree were wooden steps that the boys used to gain access to the upper levels of the tree. After climbing about twenty feet, they came to a landing where the tree limbs split, allowing the climbers to stand up and look around. "You can see downtown Pittsburgh from here," Daniel said, pointing in the direction of the city. The city looked marvelous from this vantage point on the tree. It was hard to believe that Adam passed through that city only yesterday.

The boys continued to climb to another landing where serval wooden planks had been nailed to the tree again. "Here's our tree house," Daniel said proudly. "What do you think?"

The treehouse was nothing to write home about, repeating to himself a phrase his father used often. "Nice," Adam responded, looking down to see where his two younger brothers were. He had hoped that they would not follow him up this tree and was glad to see them playing at the foot of the tree in what appeared to be a puddle of water.

"Let's go, boys. We're going for a walk," Daniel heard his father yell.

"Okay, Dad, we'll be right down." The boys looked down from their perch high above the Pittsburgh and Polish Hill landscape. "Be careful," Daniel warned Adam. "My dad will kill me if you fall and hurt yourself."

Adam was not too concerned. He was used to climbing the trees in the apple orchard next to his home but still remained cautious as he descended from the makeshift treehouse to the ground below.

Adam gathered his two brothers, and together with Daniel, they walked to the front of the Pryzinski house, where their fathers were waiting for them. On the porch stood his mom and Mrs. Pryzinski. The two women were going to stay behind to begin preparing for tonight's dinner. "Have a good time, and don't eat too much before dinnertime," Mrs. Pryzinski said as the troop left to begin their trek through Polish Hill.

"I love you, boys," Adam's mom said as she blew them a kiss. She was so embarrassing.

The women stood on the front porch watching until their families disappeared down the street, then returned back into the kitchen. Tonight was going to be a potluck dinner. Each family would bring a dish that would be shared with everyone. It was kind of a Polish Hill tradition. Pauline had volunteered to make Golabki or stuffed cabbage as most non-Polish called them. Kathryn had assured Pauline that she was more than familiar with how to make this Golabki as she made it for her family almost once a week.

A large pot of water was on the stove. They would use the pot to boil the cabbage first. Three large heads of cabbage sat on the countertop, and once the water began to boil, Pauline placed two of the three inside. The pot was not big enough to boil all three heads at one time. Kathryn had grabbed a measuring cup and a container of rice. Her job would be to make the rice, which would then be combined with the ground beef. The women would then stuff the cabbage leaves with the rice and beef mixture. Stuffing the cabbage was the most difficult part of making Golabki. The stuffed cabbage was then placed into three separate glass cooking dishes covered with a tomato sauce mixture. The Golabki would then be placed in the oven at 350 degrees, covered, and baked for an hour.

The process took the women most of the entire morning, during which time they talked and got to know one another better. Pauline began to feel a sense of friendship that she had not had before with another woman. As trust grew with her newfound friend, Pauline suddenly felt compelled to talk to Kathryn about her husband, his drinking problems, and their marriage. Her newfound courage made Pauline suddenly explode in uncontrolled sobbing and crying.

"What's the matter, Pauline?" Kathryn asked in a comforting tone of voice.

Pauline could no longer control her emotions and, with no compunctions, began to tell Kathryn everything. "He was such a good man before he started to drink, then everything changed. It's been a living hell these past few years. I'm trying desperately to keep this family together, but right now, I don't know what to do." Years of pent-up anger and stress erupted inside of Pauline as she continued to speak with Kathryn. This was the first time she had ever spoken to anyone about her problems, and it gave her a much-needed sense of relief.

Kathryn grabbed Pauline and hugged her close to her body. She knew firsthand that doing the hard work of coal-mining and steel-making placed a lot of stress on a man. She was fortunate that her husband hadn't turned to drink but knew many other wives who weren't so lucky. "Now, now, Pauline try to get yourself together. Have you tried to get Peter any help?"

"No, he won't even acknowledge that he has a drinking problem." Pauline responded. "He promised me that he would stop drinking while you folks are visiting. So far, he's kept his word. It's been a pleasure to see him sober for this long. I'm afraid that once you leave, he'll go back to drinking again."

Kathryn turned to Pauline and pushed her away enough to help wipe the tears from her eyes. "Is there anything you'd like me to do or say to Peter while we're here?" Kathryn asked.

"I think that would make things worse. I'm so grateful that I was able to finally tell someone I don't know, but please keep it a secret, just between us."

Kathryn looked again and promised that she would keep it a secret but knew that probably wasn't the best thing to do. This woman and her husband needed help that she was not equipped to provide. "Okay, dry your eyes and let's get back to work. I'll keep you and Peter in my prayers, and if you ever need to reach out to me, you can just call me any time after we leaves to go home."

Pauline looked at her friend. Even though they were of the same age, Pauline felt like she was speaking with her own mother; she was so kind and understanding.

*****

It was about 6:00 p.m. when the doorbell rang. Their dinner guests were beginning to arrive. Kathryn and Ben were in the dining room, arranging the place setting, when they were greeted by the familiar voice of Dr. Tom and his wife, Ann. "Oh my god, I didn't realize that you were coming to dinner tonight.," Kathryn said as she gave both a welcoming big hug. "What a surprise. Are you staying nearby?"

As it turned out, Tom and his wife were staying with a family only two houses down the street. "Yes, we're staying with the Walkos family. They're very nice people. It's just the four of us. They don't have kids," Dr. Tom explained. "What a great idea to get together for this dinner. We've been making pierogi all afternoon."

Kathryn was impressed. Ann Slevic was well known in the parish of being a great cook, and her pierogi were to die for.

Shortly afterward, another foursome joined the party, carrying with them kielbasa and potato pancakes and a box containing bottles of various different wines and liquors. Kathryn gave Pauline a fearful glance as she began to remove the contents of the box onto the kitchen table. Pauline gave no outward signs of distress. This was obviously going to be a major test to see if her husband would take anything to drink during dinner.

To both women's relief, the dinner celebration went on without a hitch, with Peter Pryzinski keeping his word. He had nothing to drink that night, even when a toast was made to celebrate the opening of the Polish Festival. It was around eight when Peter reminded everyone that it was time to walk over to the Parish Hall for the dance party. "We'll clean up later," Peter said. "I've been looking forward to doing some dancing all week. Besides, we need to do something to work off all of this good food."

Pauline looked at her husband with apprehension. He had not mentioned one word to her about the dance party, so she was a little taken back when he grabbed her and began dancing with her in the living room in front of all their guests. *What has gotten into this guy?* she wondered but was grateful for his sudden attention.

It was only a short walk to the Parish Hall. Pauline and Peter were the last to leave the house and were walking down the front porch steps, when Peter suddenly grabbed Pauline's hand and brought her closer to him. Neither said a word as they walked behind the others. The boys were leading the way up the hill, excited about spending time at the carnival while the adults were dancing. It was a warm summer evening, but Pauline felt compelled to grab her husband's arm and sidle up close to him. It had been a long time since she had held his hand and arm. It made her feel like a young girl again.

The dance party was in full session when the couples entered the hall. There had to be over a hundred couples already there, dancing to some newfangled rock and roll music. Peter and Ben had given their boys money, instructing them to behave and not to spend all of it at one time. "Make it last," were their last words of advice.

Pauline introduced Ben and Kathryn to Father Damian and several other committee members before turning to her husband. "Do you want to dance," she said to him, holding out an arm.

"You bet I do." Peter grabbed her and pulled her into his body. Before she realized, Peter Pryzinski was carrying and lifting her across the dance floor with grace she never knew he had.

They danced nonstop for what seemed like hours. Pauline had lost all track of time, but it didn't matter. She was back in the arms of the man she loved and married, and it felt good. She didn't want it to end. "Let's take a break and get some fresh air," Peter finally said he had walked his wife to the front door. The warm air felt good as they walked outside toward the street below. When they got near to a lamppost, Peter stopped. There in front of him was the bench they sat on years ago when they first fell in love. "Remember this bench?" Peter asked his wife as they sat down. Pauline didn't need to respond as she snuggled closer to Peter. "I know that I haven't been the best husband for you, but I wanted you to know that I still love you very much. These past serval days have made me remember all of the great times we've had together. I'm so sorry that I've hurt you."

Pauline looked into his eyes with a longing she hadn't felt in years. "Oh, Peter, I love you so much as well. I know you're a good man and father. I just want to go back to the way things were."

Without saying a word, the two embraced one another and began to kiss.

Chapter 24

The Doubleheader

The week of the Polish festival went quicker than expected for the Pryzinski family and their guests. Daniel and Adam were quickly becoming best friends and were inseparable the entire week. Daniel taught Adam everything he knew about the game of baseball. One night, they listened to an entire radio broadcast of a Pirates game on a small radio in Daniel's room. That gave Daniel the opportunity to teach Adam how to keep score. As a result, Adam's interest in the game continued to grow.

Daniel took Adam and his two younger brothers to a local playground that had a baseball diamond where the kids in the neighborhood would go to play a pickup game of baseball. Daniel had lent Adam his extra baseball glove, and the two would spend the entire afternoon playing catch and fielding groundballs. To his surprise, Adam learned that he was good at catching and fielding. On one afternoon, a group of other kids showed up and invited Daniel and Adam to play a game of baseball.

"You can play right field," Daniel told his friend before the game began. "No one hits to right field, so you shouldn't see much action out there."

Adam looked at Daniel with questioning eyes, making Daniel realize that he hadn't clearly taught Adam the various positions on a baseball field. "Right field is over there." He pointed in the direction of the right field. "First base is here, this is second base," Daniel continued until he had covered all the bases on the field.

Adam was still confused but, without saying anything, grabbed his glove and ran out to right field. During the game, only one ball was hit in his direction. As the ball took flight from the hitter's bat, Adam instinctively ran to the ball, settled underneath, opened his glove, and caught the ball. "Nice catch, Adam," he could hear his friend yell as Daniel threw the ball back into the nearest teammate.

Adam's confidence grew as the game continued. He began to understand more about the rules of baseball that he were taught by Daniel. It's a lot easier learning when you are actually playing, Adam began to learn. Batting was an entirely different story, however, as Adam struck out all three times he came to the plate, much to the dismay of his teammates. Before he knew it, the game was over, with all participants shaking hands and promising to meet again soon. Adam grabbed his glove and walked over to Daniel.

"That was a lot of fun," he said, patting his friend on the back. "I'm really starting to love this game."

Daniel smiled and looked and Adam. "Let's get going. It's almost dinnertime."

The two gathered the younger Brodziak brothers, who had been playing in a nearby mound of dirt and left the playground. Daniel was proud of his new friend and was even more excited that he had gotten him to start loving baseball, the greatest of all sports.

The rest of the week went by quickly as well for the two mothers, who themselves began to develop a close friendship. One day, the two took a bus to downtown Pittsburgh to do some shopping. During the ride, Pauline took the opportunity to tell Kathryn everything that happened the night of the adult-only dance. Pauline was like a schoolgirl describing her first kiss, when she told Kathryn how her and her husband had kissed and told her how sorry she he was. "Maybe all of my prayers are finally being answered," Pauline hopefully said.

"I've been praying a Rosary for you and Peter, every night before I go to bed," Kathryn responded. "I just know everything is going to work out for you two. God will find a way."

The men had also found a way to get to know one another better. Although Peter had taken the week off, he took the opportunity to take Ben to the steel mill plant where he worked. Ben was amazed when he entered the plant. The noise was deafening, and the smell from the smoke made his nose sting and eyes water. Working underneath the ground in a coal mine was dangerous work, but for once, he was glad that he had chosen that profession over working in a steel mill.

Peter introduced Ben to his foreman and to the rest of the crew and told them that he was a coal miner from Windber, Pennsylvania. "If you ever get tired of working the mines, we can always find you a job with us," said Peter's foreman as the two left after two hours of touring the mill.

No, thanks, Ben thought, *I'll stay where I'm at*, glad to finally leave the noisy and smelly plant. As they walked through the front gate, Ben noticed hundreds of train cars loaded full of coal. On the nearby Allegheny River, he also saw barges loaded full of coal. He wondered if any of this was Windber coal. It made Ben realize how closely the two industries were tied to one another and how essential they were to the economies of the area where they lived and worked.

At night, following dinner, the two families would venture out onto the streets of Polish hill, where they would lesson to polka bands and sample all kinds of ethnic foods from the food trucks parked along the way. The center of the festival was the carnival. The last Saturday of the festival was designated as "family night" at the carnival, where the price of all ride tickets was halved. It was while they were walking through the carnival grounds that Peter and Pauline ran into George Zanecky.

"Hello, Pauline. Hello, Peter," George greeted the couple. "Are you guys having a fun time? Where are the kids? I know that they have to be having a great time. How could you not?" he said before catching his breath. "What a success this festival has been. We have people coming into Polish Hill from everywhere. You two are hosting a family, if I recall." Before either could respond, George continued, "Do you like the Pirates tickets I got for you, Peter?"

Peter looked at his wife. She had neglected to tell her husband that she had gotten free tickets from George. "We can't wait to go tomorrow. The boys are really excited. I haven't been to a game all season," Peter responded without actually thanking him. He never liked George. He knew that he had dated Pauline before they were married, so he felt some degree of jealousy toward the man. Besides, he was a lawyer who didn't really know what it was like to do hard work for a living. His assessment of George was unfounded as he knew that George had helped many of the union men with their disability claims when they got injured on the job. Regardless, Peter could not overcome his sense of resentment toward this man.

"I didn't know that he got us the tickets to the Pirates game," he told his wife after George had walked away.

"It must have slipped my mind," Pauline quickly responded.

"I really don't like that guy, Pauline. I would have liked to have bought my own tickets."

"He was just trying to be nice, and it was his way of thanking me for helping him with the festival committee."

Peter dropped Pauline's hand he had been holding the entire night. The two said little to one another until they got home later on that evening.

*****

Sunday, July 17, 1960, was the start of what appeared to be a beautiful day. Adam and Daniel would be going with their fathers to the Pirates doubleheader that day at Forbes Field. The first game was scheduled to begin at 1:05 p.m. In addition to Daniel, Adam, and their fathers, Daniel's two older brothers would also be going to the game. Adam's two younger brothers would be staying home with their mother and Mrs. Pryzinski. The plan was for both families to attend ten o'clock Mass before going to the game. After Mass, a bus would take them from Immaculate Heart of Mary Church to Forbes Field.

Daniel could not contain his excitement and could hardly wait for Mass to end. His mother had packed him a lunch, which he had placed in the back of his school backpack along with two baseball gloves, one for him and one for Adam, and two scorebooks the boys would use to keep score. The Pirates were currently in first place in the National League and were favored to win both games. The Pirates' ace, Vernon Law, would be starting for the Pirates in the first game. He was leading the NL with a pitching record of 11–5.

As Father Damian gave his final blessing with the sign of the cross over his congregation, he concluded by asking God's help for the Pirates to win today's games. Following the final blessing, Adam and Daniel raced down the steps of the church where buses were waiting to take them to the game. "Wait up, boys! We all want to go together, so let's all get on the same bus," Mr. Pryzinski instructed.

"Hurry up, Dad! We want to get there sometime today," Daniel responded sarcastically.

Both families got onto the first bus in line. Daniel insisted that they sit up front to ensure that they would be the first ones off when they got to the field.

The ride to Forbes Field from the church took only fifteen minutes, but for Daniel, it seemed like forever. Adam sat next to his friend during the short ride and was sitting next to the window and was the first one to see Forbes Field as the bus drew closer. As the bus pulled to its designated parking spot directly next to the ballpark, it was an amazing site for Adam to see. He hadn't expected it to be so big. Hundreds of people were walking on the sidewalk toward what appeared to be the front entrances.

"Let's go!" Daniel yelled once the doors to the bus were opened.

Before they could leave, the bus driver stood up, blocking everyone's exit. "Before you folks leave, I want you all to remember that this is bus number 101. I will be waiting for you here at this same spot once the games are over to take you back to church. If anyone gets lost, just follow the crowds to the bus parking spot, and you should have no problem finding this bus. We have a full bus, so I won't leave until everyone gets back. Have a great day, have fun, and 'Beat 'Em, Bucs.'"

Everyone in the bus gave a hardy yell, repeating the same familiar refrain of "Beat 'Em, Bucs!"

Once they regrouped outside the bus, Peter Pryzinski looked around and then looked at the tickets we was holding in his hand. "This way." Daniel looked at his father, not sure that he knew exactly where he was going but followed him anyway. As they arrived at the front gate vendors were yelling, "Get your programs here." Others were selling pennants with the Pittsburgh Pirates logo. Others were selling Pirates T-shirts and baseball caps. Adam felt overwhelmed, wondering if his dad was going to purchase any of these items. Before going inside, Peter Pryzinski stopped and began to give each one of them their own ticket.

"Stay close now and meet together once we get inside." The group followed him obediently as they entered the gate to the ball-park. Once inside, they regrouped, standing directly behind Peter who again was looking for their next direction of travel. "Everyone is here. Let's go this way." Continuing to believe that his father knew where he was going, Daniel followed with the rest until they reached at sign above which read Pirates' dugout. One by one, they entered into the brilliant sunlight and green grass of Forbes Field. Daniel was taken back. It looked like they would be sitting directly behind the Pirates dugout. He looked quickly at his tickets. His seat was in row 10. As he followed his father down the steps, they got closer and closer to the playing field until they reached row 10. He couldn't believe it! Their seats were only 10 rows behind the Pirates' dugout. How did his dad manage to get such great seats? Daniel wondered as he finally sat down on seat number 9. Adam sat next to him and looked at Daniel with amazement. "These seats are great!" he told his friend.

Adam looked around and for the first time in his life was able to see what a Major League Baseball Park looked like. Below him on the field, he could see the black-and-gold uniforms of the Pittsburgh Pirates players and the Red and White unform of the Cincinnati Reds. "There's Bill Mazeroski," Daniel said with excitement. For the past week, Adam heard of no one else but Bill Mazeroski and knew that he was Daniel favorite player. Adam was hoping that Maz would play well today.

Suddenly, the boy's thoughts were interrupted by the public address announcer who was announcing to the audience, "Now for today's starting lineups."

"Oh my gosh, I nearly forgot," Daniel said he grabbed his backpack. "We need to enter the starting lineups in our scorebooks." Reaching inside, he retrieved the two scorebooks and the two pencils he had stored there, just as the announcer started giving the names of today's starting lineups. The boys listened carefully and wrote the names in their respective books. When the announcer had finished, they looked at entries. Both had recorded the same names:

For the Reds

1 Eddie Kasko: 3B
2 Vada Pinson: CF
3 Gus Bell: RF
4 Wally Post: LF
5 Frank Robinson: 1B
6 Ed Bailey: C
7 Roy McMillan: SS
8 Billy Martin: 2B
9 Bob Purkey: P

For the Pirates

1 Bill Virdon: CF
2 Dick Groat: SS
3 Bob Skinner: LF
4 Rocky Nelson: 1B
5 Roberto Clemente: RF
6 Hal Smith: C
7 Don Hoak: 3B
8 Bill Mazeroski: 2B
9 Vern Law: P

Now they were ready to watch the game. Daniel was wearing his baseball glove in his left hand and was trying to hold the score-card and pencil in this right hand. After realizing that he could not do both, he took off his glove. "If a foul ball comes back at us, we're have to catch it barehanded."

Adam hadn't even thought about catching a foul ball. What would be the odds of him catching a foul ball anyway? Suddenly the boys heard the familiar cry from the home plate umpire, "Play ball!" and the game was underway.

The game was scoreless until the top of the 5th inning when the Reds scored 1 run on 4 hits and led the game 1–0. The Reds really broke the game wide open in the top of the sixth inning when they scored 5 runs on 6 hits and lead the Pirates 6–0. This was enough to chase starter Law from the game and was replaced by relief pitcher, Fred Green. The Pirates were able to score 1 run on 2 hits in the bottom of the sixth but still trailed the Reds 6–1. The Pirates finally came to life in the bottom of the eighth inning when they scored 4 runs on 5 hits and 1 error by the Reds. During this inning one of the Pirates, young hitter, Roberto Clemente, fouled off several pitches. Adam was paying more attention to his scorebook than to the field when one the foul balls flew right at him. The ball hit a seat in front of him and bounded into the air and landed directly on his lap. Daniel screamed as Adam retrieved the ball from his lap. He actually had caught a foul ball.

Everyone around him was yelling and patting him on the back. His dad was sitting directly behind him. "Way to go, son!" he said proudly. "That's a souvenir you'll be able to keep forever."

Adam turned to his friend, feeling a little guilty about catching the ball. "Here you go, Daniel, you have it. I know how much you wanted to catch a foul ball today." Daniel looked at his friend as he handed the ball to him.

"Are you sure you don't want to keep it? It's not often you catch a foul ball!"

"I'm sure, Daniel, you've been so good to me this entire week. This is my thanks to you." Daniel reached over and hugged his friend.

0

The crowd around them, realizing what was happening, stood and applauded Daniel. "Gee, kid, that's awfully nice of you," one nearby spectator said.

The Pirates went on to lose the first game of the doubleheader by a final score of 6–5, but neither boy, especially Daniel, seemed to care. In his hand, he held a baseball that had been fouled off by the great Roberto Clemente. More importantly, the kind gesture from Adam would seal their friendship forever.

In between games, the boys decided to try to get as many autographs on their new baseball from as many Pirates as possible. After a short break, the Pirates came back onto the playing field to warm up, which gave them the ideal opportunity to try and get one of the players to sign it. Adam stood on the railing next to the dugout and yelled to Bill Mazeroski, trying to get his attention and to sign the baseball. Bill finally looked in his direction and walked slowly toward Adam. Before he could say anything, Adam grabbed the ball from Daniel and handed it over to Mazeroski. Just as Bill was signing the ball, Adam could see another player out of the corner of this eye walk to where they were standing.

"Here, Bob, sign this ball for the boy."

Adam looked up to find that Roberto Clemente was now holding the ball and signing it. After Clemente signed the ball, Adam gave it back to Daniel, who stood next to him in complete shock. "You got Clemente's autograph!" Daniel said incredulously.

"Yeah, and Mazeroski's as well!" Adam said. Both boys ran back to their seats.

"Look whose autographs we got," said Daniel has he held up the ball, not wanting anyone else to touch it.

"Good job, boys," Peter Pryzinski said. Adam could hear a slight slur in Peter's voice that he hadn't heard before and was wondering if Daniel's father was feeling all right. Standing next to his father was Dr. Tom and his wife, Ann. They had taken the same bus over with them to the game, but in his excitement, Adam hadn't noticed.

"That was very nice of you, Adam, to give the foul ball to your friend," Dr. Tom said as he patted Adam on the shoulder.

Adam just smiled back at the doctor. *It was no big deal*, Adam thought.

The second game of the doubleheader began shortly afterward, and the sellout crowd quickly took their seats when the first pitch was thrown. Tom Cheney was starting for the Pirates. This was only his third start of the season, so expectations were not as high as in the first game. To everyone's surprise, Tom ended up pitching a nine-inning shutout against the Reds and won the game 5–0. The Pirates scored 5 runs on 14 hits while earning the win. Cheney gave up only four hits to the Reds to earn the win and to improve his record to 2–1.

During the game, however, Adam began to notice a change in Mr. Pryzinski. He became louder and louder as the game progressed and at times began yelling at the Reds players when they came to bat. At the same time, Adam began to notice that Daniel had gotten very quiet and had become withdrawn. Halfway through the game, Adam noticed that his friend had stopped keeping score. He had lost all his previous excitement about the game and appeared to be frightened. "What's wrong with you? Are you feeling okay? The Pirates are winning. You should be happy," Adam said, trying to boost his friend's spirits. Adam glimpsed back at his dad, who just shook his head at him. *What's going on around here?* Adam wondered. *What is wrong with everyone?*

The game ended when Frank Robinson of the Reds popped out to the Pirates shortstop, Dick Groat. Daniel was the only one in their group who stood up and applauded. Adam turned around to see Mr. Pryzinski fast asleep in his seat. Dr. Tom and his dad were sitting next to him, trying to wake him up. "What's wrong with your dad?" Adam said to Daniel.

"He's drunk," Daniel replied. Daniel's older brother Mike had slid next to them in an empty seat.

"My dad gets drunk a lot," said Mike.

Daniel reached over and struck his brother on the arm. "Shut up, Mike!" was all Daniel could say.

Adam felt confused and a little frightened. He wasn't sure exactly what being drunk meant.

"He's been drinking beer ever since the seventh inning of the first game," Mike said. "He must have had ten beers. I tried to get him to stop, but he wouldn't listen to me. He never does." Adam looked at his father in hopes of getting an answer and easing his concerns over Mr. Pryzinski. He had not known the man long but liked him very much.

"He's going to be fine, Adam. He's just had a little too much beer. Dr. Tom and I will help him to get back onto the bus."

The two men grabbed Peter by each arm and pulled him up from his seat. The man could not stand on his own and nearly fell down over the seat in front of him.

"Let's go, Peter. We need to get you home. A little rest and some coffee will help to sober you up," said Dr. Tom. After much struggle, they were finally able to walk Peter to the landing over where they were sitting. Slowly, Peter began to walk on his own but needed the support of Ben and Dr. Tom to walk the distance back to the bus.

"I was getting worried about you folks. I was beginning to think that you had decided to walk home. What have he here?" the bus driver said after taking one look at Peter Pryzinski.

"I'm a doctor," said Dr. Tom, "and this man has had too much to drink. We need to get him home as soon as possible."

"Okay, Doc, whatever you say. Get him to sit down, and we'll be on our way."

As soon as they were able to get Peter to sit down in the first seat that was open, the bus driver closed the bus and was on his way. Hardly anyone on the bus had noticed that Peter was drunk. By now, most of the traffic from the game had cleared so getting back to Immaculate Heart of Mary Church was quicker than expected. The bus driver was kind enough to drop off the other passengers in the bus before he offered to drop their group off directly in front of the Pryzinski home. "I was hoping to get this guy home without embarrassing him in front of the other passengers," the driver said with sympathy.

"Thanks. That was very kind of you," Adam's father said in response. "Their family appreciates it."

"Okay, big guy, we're home. Time to wake up and get off this bus." Peter Pryzinski struggled to regain his feet as they attempted to get him up and off the bus. After some effort, they managed to get Peter off the bus. As they began to walk him up the front steps of the Pryzinski home, Pauline came running to greet them.

"What have you done, Peter? You've been doing so well. How could you embarrass us like this in front of all these strangers?" She began to cry as Peter stumbled up to the porch and through the front door. As soon as he got into the kitchen, Peter stumbled forward and with a loud thud hit the floor and passed out underneath the kitchen table. "I'm so sorry. I'm so embarrassed. He had promised not to drink until you folks had left to go home. He was doing so well." Pauline was now crying uncontrollably.

"Kids, go upstairs for a while as we get things sorted out here," Adam's father demanded.

All the boys, including Michael, obeyed and walked upstairs. Mike knew that it was going to be a long night.

"I don't know what to say," Pauline sobbed. "He's really a good man when he's not drinking."

Adam's mother quickly interrupted, "Pauline, you need to listen to me and listen to me good. I know that you didn't want me to say anything to anyone, but your husband needs help. You can't continue to ignore this. It's not good for you or your family as long has he continues to have this problem." She glanced over to Dr. Slevic who was standing in the kitchen next to his wife. "Doctor, what can we do for this man? Can you get him admitted to the Somerset County Alcohol rehab center?"

Dr. Tom looked at Kathryn, then to Pauline who was still standing near her fallen husband, crying. "First of all, Peter's going to have to want to go into the rehabilitation center voluntarily. I can't force him if he doesn't want to go. Secondly, the program requires that he spend thirty days minimum in order to maximize his recovery. During that time, he can't see anyone. No family or friends. I may be able to have Pauline visit, but it would have to be for a short period of time, and once a week if we're lucky. Third, Peter will have to start attending weekly Alcoholic Anonymous meetings, along with psychiatric counseling. Lastly, the center is a two-hour drive from his home here in Pittsburgh. There must be a closer facility."

Kathryn looked at the doctor and spoke, "If we can get him to agree to attend the center in Somerset, Pauline and her family can stay with us the entire time, whatever it takes. I think Peter needs to get away from this place for a while. Going to Somerset may be the best thing for him."

Pauline had slowly regained her composure and looked at Kathryn. "I'm willing to do whatever it takes to convince Peter to go to rehab. I'll give him no alternative. It's either he goes or I leave him, and I'll take the boys with me. The two older boys can stay with their grandparents, so I'll only have to take Daniel with me to stay with your family, if that's okay with you, Kathryn."

Kathryn Brodziak reached over and hugged her friend. "You and your family are more than welcome to stay with us as long as it takes." She looked over to her husband, who was nodding his head in agreement.

They all looked at Peter, who was passed out on the floor. "Let him sleep it off tonight, Pauline," Dr. Tom said. "It sounds like you already know the drill. If he agrees, I'll call the rehab center tomorrow and make arrangements to have him admitted."

Chapter 25

Rehabilitation

Peter opened his eyes and quickly sat up. What was he doing lying on the kitchen floor? His head was pounding as he tried to get up from the floor. In the living room, he could see the dim light of a lamp that was sitting next to the couch on a table. After focusing his eyes, he could see his wife sitting on the couch, wide awake, and looking out to the front window. "Pauline, I need help," Peter said as he grabbed the top of the kitchen table for support.

Pauline turned and looked in the direction of the kitchen and got up to help her husband. "Come on, Peter, you've been laying there all night. Go and lie down on the couch, and I'll get you a couple of aspirins." After getting her husband onto the couch and covering him with a blanket, she returned shortly afterward with a glass of water in her hand. "Here, drink this and take these aspirins. It'll make your head feel better."

Peter complied, sheepishly looking at his wife. He knew that he was in trouble with her but didn't know exactly what to say. "How did I get home from the game yesterday?" he finally asked his wife.

"Don't worry about that just yet. Just lay down and get some rest. We'll talk more in the morning." The anger and embarrassment she had felt against her husband had all but vanished. All she wanted to do right now was to try to get him help. She pulled the blanket over him as he lay on the couch and bent down and gave him a kiss on the forehead. "I'm going to get you fixed, no matter what it was going to take," Pauline said to herself as her husband closed his eyes and fell asleep.

Before leaving for that night, Dr. Tom and Ann and Ben and Kathryn all agreed that they would all meet in the morning to help Pauline as part of an intervention of sorts to try to get Peter to agree to admit himself into an alcohol rehabilitation program. Before he and Kathryn went upstairs to bed, Ben turned to Pauline. "It was all my fault, Pauline. I didn't know Peter had a drinking problem. I'm the one who bought him his first beer at the ball game. I was so proud that the boys caught a foul ball that I wanted to celebrate. Peter was sitting next to me, so I bought him a beer. Before I knew it, one beer led to another. I tried to stop him, but Peter wouldn't listen. Before I knew it, Peter was passed out in his seat."

"Don't blame yourself Ben. It wasn't your fault. Peter is a grown man and needs to learn to control himself. I've been dealing with his drinking problem for years and really haven't told anyone until now. It was meant to be, I guess, that you folks are here with us now. Maybe Peter will finally agree to get help."

*****

It was about 10:00 a.m. when the doorbell rang. Pauline opened the door and was greeted by Dr. Tom and Ann. "How's he doing?" Tom asked with concern in his voice. "We didn't get much sleep last night, thinking about everything that happened."

"He's awake and in the kitchen, having some coffee. He's still hungover," Pauline said as she walked them into the kitchen.

Peter was sitting at the kitchen table along with Ben and Kathryn. No one was really saying anything, making for an awkward silence. Before getting to the Pryzinski home this morning, Dr. Tom decided to handle the matter using a physician's rather than a friend's approach. So Tom was the first to speak to Peter and spoke to him as though he were a patient. "Listen, Peter, drinking too much is bad for your health. It can lead to all kinds of health problems, like cirrhosis of the liver, heart disease, and cancer. As a doctor, I highly recommend that you do something to control your drinking. From what Pauline has said, you've been drinking a lot for the past several years. It's starting to pay a toll on her and your boys as well."

Before Dr. Tom could say any more, Kathryn interrupted, "Dr. Tom works at a marvelous rehabilitation facility in Somerset, Pennsylvania. If you want, he can help to get you admitted into the program, but you're going to want to do it on your own. We can't force you if you don't want to."

Looking around the table at the people who were trying to help him, Peter realized that they were more than his guests. They had become friends to both him and his family. Friends he could cherish and trust more than anything. Peter looked at Pauline and began to cry. "I am so sorry, sweetheart! I know I let you down. I wanted nothing more but to stop drinking to make you happy. These past couple weeks made me remember what it was like to come home sober every day."

Pauline grabbed his hand and kissed it. "I know you have, Peter, but you can't do this on your own anymore. You need help from professionals who are trained to give it to you."

Peter looked at his friends, then said, "Okay, Doc, what do I need to do?"

A sense of relief filled the room as Dr. Tom explained in detail what the program was about and what was expected from Peter over the next thirty days and beyond. "Somerset is a beautiful little town not far from where we live in Windber. Pauline and the boys can stay with us and come to visit you whenever permitted. I think you'd like staying there," Kathryn said encouragingly.

"That's very kind of you and Ben," Peter said as he held Pauline's hand tightly.

Things began to happen quickly after that. Dr. Tom called his office at the rehabilitation center and made arrangements to have Peter admitted. He was somewhat pleased to find out that the center would be sending a car and driver to pick Peter up right from his home in Pittsburgh. The idea was to have a new client realize how important it was to be separated from any family or friends from the start, so the main focus was on the client's recovery from their addiction.

Pauline called her mother to let her know of their plans. Although she was at first hesitant, she agreed to allow her oldest grandsons, Michael and Luke, to stay with her while Peter was in rehab. She then called Peter's foreman to let him know of the situation. Belonging to such a powerful union as the United Steelworkers had its benefits. Under their contract, a member was given up to six months paid leave and was guaranteed his job back after returning from any type of disability, which included alcohol or drug addiction issues. His foreman would notify the union, who in turn would take care of all the paperwork.

Lastly, it was agreed that Pauline would drive their family car back to Windber with Kathryn, Daniel, and Adam. Ben would return to Windber with the other boys on the bus that took them to Pittsburgh. That bus would be leaving the Immaculate Heart of Mary Church sometime later on in the day. Dr. Tom and Ann would also be taking the same bus home. "I'll check up on you, Peter, as soon as I get back into the office on Tuesday. You should be settled in by then," Dr. Tom promised.

Pauline gathered her sons together and spoke to them alone to let them know about the plans that were made to get their father's help with his drinking problems. "I need you boys to be strong and pray for your father's recovery. This is the best thing we can do for him, but it's not going to be easy for him or us."

Michael looked at his mother and gave her a big kiss. "Don't worry, Mom, everything is going to work out okay," he said.

"I need you and Luke to behave for your grandparents while I'm away. It's going to be a long time before we see one another again, but I'll try calling you boys every day while I'm away. I wish I could take you with me, but it'll will be too much of a burden to expect the Brodziaks to allow all of us to stay with them. As I told you, Daniel will be going with me since he's the youngest," Pauline said as tears began to well up in her eyes.

Her parents lived only a couple of blocks away. The boys normally would spend most of their time during the summer months visiting their grandparents but seldom, if ever, stayed overnight. In addition to his paper route, Michael also just got a second job this summer at Zinkowski's Grocery Store, bagging groceries.

Luke was a pretty outgoing kid and spent a lot of his time playing with neighborhood friends. He was capable of taking care of himself. Pauline knew that her sons were good boys who would provide little trouble for her parents. Regardless, they had never been apart from one another, so when Pauline dropped them off in the afternoon, she could hardly maintain her emotions. "I don't know when we'll be back home again. It's going to depend on how well your father makes out." She had already told them that their father would be in rehab for at least thirty days but didn't want to remind them again. It seemed like such a long time.

They hugged and all said their goodbyes, and when she got back home, she began to pack clothes for herself, Peter, and Daniel. She packed the only suitcase they owned with Peter's clothes, a toothbrush, razors, shaving cream, and aftershave. It took all of her weight as she sat on the suitcase to get the bulging suitcase closed. Even then, she wondered if she had packed enough for her husband's lengthy stay.

Shortly after 1:00 p.m., the car from the Somerset Alcohol Rehabilitation Center arrived to pick up her husband. As he grabbed his suitcase, he turned to his wife and Daniel and hugged them both. "Guess I'll see you soon," Peter said, still uncertain as to what to expect.

Pauline looked at her husband and said, "Good luck, Peter. We'll come to see you as soon as we can. I love you."

Daniel looked at his dad, then gave him a final hug before he left. "Love you, Dad. Get well," was all Daniel could say as he followed his dad to the waiting car. Both Pauline and Daniel stood on the sidewalk and followed that car until it disappeared down the street.

Kathryn Brodziak and Adam were waiting for them inside the house and greeted them. Kathryn didn't know what to expect was going to happen to them all over the next thirty days but had resolved to do whatever it took to make her friends feel at home with her and her family once they got back home to Windber. Ben and her other kids had caught the bus home earlier, so now it was just the four of them waiting their turn to journey back to Windber. "Do you think you've taken care of everything here?" Kathryn asked Pauline. She was anxious to get underway but didn't want to rush her friend.

"I think so, but if I've forgotten anything, I'll just call my mom. She has the key to the house and promised to check in while we're away. I guess we need to get moving," Pauline said with reluctance in her voice.

The Chevrolet Impala was parked on the street in front of the Pryzinski house. It had been a while since she had driven it but felt confident as she opened the front door and got behind the wheel. Kathryn sat next to her in the front seat, and the two boys fit comfortably in the back. It was warm outside, and the interior of the car was even hotter. "Open the windows, everyone, until I get the air conditioner turned on. It'll cool things off quickly."

Kathryn looked at her, impressed. Their Ford Falcon didn't have air-conditioning. "Do you know how to get to the turnpike from here. I thought it would be the fastest way for us to go, but we'll have to pay the tolls."

Pauline responded by informing Kathryn that she had planned to take Route 30. She had inspected a travel map earlier and noticed that Route 30 was a toll-free road that they could take all the way from Greensburg to Somerset.

"I've never gone that way, but you're the driver and it's your car."

Pauline smiled and handed over the travel map to her front seat passenger. "Take a look, and you can help me with directions." With that, the foursome took off on their way east to Somerset County and the towns of Somerset and Windber.

Route 30, as it was now called, is the original Lincoln Highway that was constructed in the early 1900s to provide automobile travelers with a highway that ran from Broadway in New York City in the east to San Francisco in the west. The road was named in honor of the fifteenth president, Abraham Lincoln. Following the main road from Pittsburgh, Pauline was able to catch Route 30 near Greensburg, Pennsylvania. From there, it was a straight drive to Somerset. As they approached Latrobe, the rolling hills of the Laurel Highlands of western Pennsylvania made for a very picturesque drive as the foursome traveled from one small town and village to the next.

When they stopped for ice cream at the town to Ligonier, Kathryn consulted the map. She didn't know exactly what Pauline wanted to do. From Ligonier, they could drive north over the mountains to Johnstown or continue straight to Somerset. "Pauline, can I suggest something? It's getting late, and we're all getting tired. I think the best thing we could do today is to drive to my house in Windber. From here, we can go north and be there in about forty-five minutes to an hour. Going to Somerset first will take us an hour out of our way. According to Dr. Tom, you won't be able to see Peter today anyway. Why don't we go to my house now and we can decide what we want to do tomorrow?"

Pauline looked at her friend, then together, they consulted the map. Kathryn pointed to their current location, then followed the road leading north to Johnstown. Kathryn did the same thing, showing the direction they would take to Somerset, then the distance from Somerset to Windber. Pauline had hoped she would be able to see her husband today before Kathryn reminded her of the visitation restrictions Dr. Tom had discussed. After some lengthy discussions, the two women agreed that the best thing would be to go to Windber first.

"Do you want me to drive?" Kathryn offered, knowing full well that her friend must be exhausted after such a long day. "Once we get over this mountain, I think I know the way from there. At least we'll be close and could always stop for directions."

With a sense of relief, Pauline agreed to allow Kathryn to drive the rest of the way. Until they had stopped, Pauline hadn't realized how tired she was.

It took a little over an hour to drive from Ligonier to Windber. During that time, Pauline fell fast asleep while the boys sat quietly behind them. The road signs provided adequate and timely directions and eventually placed them onto Route 56, just ten miles west of Windber. From there, they were home in ten minutes. As they pulled into the driveway, Pauline woke up and said, "Are we here?"

The boys couldn't contain their excitement and ran from the car before Kathryn had a chance to turn off the ignition.

"Yes, we're home," Kathryn said to herself. It had been only a week since they had left, but for now, it felt like an eternity. So much had happened during that time, and Kathryn knew that there was much more to come.

Chapter 26

Life in a Small Town

Growing up in a small, rural town like Windber can provide a young boy with plenty of things to do free from the constraints that boys have growing up in the big city. A guy can walk anywhere and not be afraid of getting mugged or beaten up. In a small town, everyone knows one another, and they look out for each other. There is no concern about just walking up to someone's house and knocking on the front door if you're looking for help. Strong family and religious beliefs are the constants that combine to help make small town living a peaceful and safe place to grow up. So when Pauline and Daniel Pryzinski joined their small-town family to live in the summer of 1960, they quickly learned that the Brodziak family was very accommodating and welcomed them as they would their own family.

Shortly after their arrival, Adam had taken Daniel into town to show him around. The main street of Windber ran for only two miles from one end to the other, and it took less than twenty minutes for the boys to walk to the center of town. Other than the Arcadia Movie Theatre and the fire station, there really wasn't much to see. In the center of town was a train station, but according to Adam, few trains stopped there. Last year, his school took a train ride to Altoona to see the circus. That was the last time Adam remembered seeing a passenger train pass through town. Most of the trains moving through nowadays were carrying coal from the local mines in the area to places like Pittsburgh and Cleveland in the west.

After showing him the town, the boys stopped at Anderson's on the way back home. Anderson's was a novelty store located in town that also served as a newsstand. The store sold a large variety of penny candy, so every kid in town loved to stop there. With the money they got from their parents, Adam and Daniel got their fill of candy before heading home.

It was still early afternoon when the boys got back from their walk about town. "Let's play catch," Daniel said to Adam. Playing catch would become part of their daily routine. Daniel would throw the ball high in the air, teaching Adam the art of catching fly balls. Then he would throw sharp ground balls at Adam, often forcing him to make diving stops. All the while, their skills at playing baseball improved with each passing day.

The Brodziak backyard was over an acre and big enough to hold an entire baseball field. The yard backed up to a large forest on one side and a farm on the other. Next to the house was an orchard of apple, plum, pear, and cherry trees. The boys would climb the big apple tree located at the far end of the orchard and sit there for hours, talking about things but mostly baseball.

One day, shortly after they got out of bed in the morning, Adam asked Daniel, "Do you want to milk a cow today city boy?"

Daniel looked at his friend, unsure how to respond. He'd never seen a cow before, let alone milk one. "Sure. Why not?" Daniel responded with some trepidation.

After breakfast, Adam told his mom, "I'm taking Daniel over to McGovern's farm to help herd the cows into the barn and to see if John will let us milk them today."

John was the farm's hired hand, who was always glad to receive a helping hand handling the herd. "Okay, but be careful," Kathryn said as the boys exited the rear door near the kitchen.

"Do you think they'll be okay?" Pauline asked after they left.

"Adam and his brothers have been helping over the farm for the past couple of summers now. It gives them something to do. Besides, farming teaches you a lot about hard work and dedication."

Pauline looked at her friend with some skepticism but said nothing more as she watched her son from the rear window of the kitchen. This is something new that she had not expected her son would ever have the opportunity to do if he had stayed home in Pittsburgh.

The two friends walked to the barbed wire fence that separated the Brodziak property from the dairy farm pasture. "Crawl underneath but be careful. The barbed wire can really hurt if you get stuck on it." Adam lifted the lower wire high enough to let his friend move underneath. Adam followed, and before they knew it, the two were on the other side of the fence, walking in the pasture. "John takes the cows to the upper paster early in the morning. The grazing is better up there," Adam advised Daniel.

As the boys began their hike, Daniel looked up in the direction they were walking. The upper pasture was located on a high hill located directly behind the barn. The boys would have to walk to the top of the hill to reach the upper pasture. When they got to the top, Daniel turned around and was amazed by the view. Western Pennsylvania was noted for its rolling hills, and in every direction from their vantage point, one could see nothing but rolling hills surrounding the small town of Windber.

"What a beautiful view," Daniel exclaimed. "We go tobogganing down this hill in the winter. My dad soaks rolls of toilet paper in kerosene and nails the rolls to stakes. He then takes the stakes and hammers them into the ground the entire length of the hill. He must have over twenty stakes in the ground. At night, when it's dark, my dad lights each roll up, and they serve like torches lighting our path down the hill. The entire town comes out to sled ride. My parents usually serve hot cider at the bottom of the hill. It's a great time. Maybe your parents will let you come out to visit us during the winter." Daniel could only image what it would be like seeing this hill covered in snow and being lit up by toilet paper torches at night.

The cows were waiting for them as they finally arrived at the area where they were grazing. Adam could see John sitting in the tractor, which was attached to a small trailer hauling bales of hay. The idea was for John to lead the cows to the barn, using hay as an enticement. "Hello, Adam. Who's our friend?" John greeted them with a friendly farmer's smile.

"His name is Daniel. He's from Pittsburgh and is staying with us for a while. I thought we'd teach him how to milk a cow today."

John looked Daniel over and said, "A city boy, hey? Well, welcome. We'll teach you what it's like living in the country. Let's get going these cows need to get milked." With that, John started his tractor and handed the boys two wood poles. "Use these to herd the cows to the barn. Most of them just follow me, but some of the younger cows haven't learned yet. So try to keep them together."

It only took twenty minutes to get the cows from the upper pasture, into the barn. The boys followed closely behind as they were instructed, making sure that the herd kept moving, trying hard not to step on manure.

When they got to the barn, Daniel was surprised to see how clean it was. Each cow seemed to know exactly where they were supposed to be as one by one, they entered into hay-covered stalls. Each stall contained a bucket of grain located on the other end of a gate. As the cow bent down to feed on the grain, John would close the gate around the neck of each cow, preventing them from moving. "Come here, son," John directed Daniel. "Have a seat on the stool, and I'll teach you how to milk a cow. Here is a bucket that you will use to catch the milk." John reached down and grabbed one of the cow's teats and began to pull on it. Milk began to squirt into the bucket with each stroke. "Now you try. Just sit here and milk. You'll know when your finished when no more milk comes out."

It took several tries before Daniel got the hang of it. His milk pail was almost full when John came over to inspect. "Looks like we'll make a farmer out of you yet."

Daniel smiled. His arm and hand were sore from milking. It had taken him twenty minutes to fill up his bucket. There had to be fifty more cows to milk. How were they ever going to milk them all. "I showed you the old-fashioned way of milking. We don't milk cows that way anymore," John said as he pulled up a device and laid it next to Daniel. "Let me show you how it works." John began by placing one of the tentacles attached to the device to each one of the cow's teats. Daniel could hear the suction as the device began to mechanically milk the next cow in line. John went on to attach similar devices to each cow, and within an hour's time, all of the cows had been milked.

"From here, we take the milk to the pasteurizing building located next to the barn, where we pasteurize the milk so it's safe to drink. Our milkmen then deliver the milk each morning to our cus-tomers," John informed both boys. "I'll release the cows from their stalls to the lower pasture where they will graze until the evening, milking."

Farming is a lot of work, Daniel thought as the boys left the barn to walk across the pasture toward the Brodziak house they could see in the distance. Daniel was hungry and exhausted and smelled like manure, but he never felt so good and alive in his entire life.

The summer rolled along quickly for the two boys as their friendship grew stronger each day. Adam continued his efforts to keep his new friend entertained, which wasn't very hard since living in a small, rural town provided young boys with plenty to do. One hot day, Adam decided to take Daniel to the Windber Recreational Park to swim in the pool. Adam had completed his swimming les-sons early in the summer before their visit to Pittsburgh and consid-ered himself to be an expert swimmer. Daniel, on the other hand, had never taken swimming lessons but was willing to learn. It was a Saturday morning when Adam took Daniel for the two-mile hike from his home through Mine 42 and up to the top of the mountain where the swimming pool was located. Daniel had not expected to walk that far, let alone have to cross a creek and climb up a mountain, so he was exhausted when they got to the park.

"You guys have a lot of hills around here," Daniel exclaimed as they sat down on a bench outside the entrance to the pool.

"It helps to keep us in shape," Adam replied. Adam's lifeguard friend, Mike, was on duty and greeted them at the front entrance. "Mike, I want you to meet my friend Daniel. He's from Pittsburgh and is staying with us during the summer."

"Welcome to Windber, Daniel. It's nice to meet you. It going to be a hot one today, so try to keep cool." The boys walked into the gated swimming pool area and changed into their swimming trunks in the men's locker room.

They found a spot on the grassy area adjacent to the pool, where they laid down the towels Adam's mother had packed for them. "Let's get wet!" Adam said as he ran to the edge of the pool and jumped in, feet first. Daniel followed closely behind but decided to sit down on the edge of the pool before sliding himself in. The water was cool but refreshing. Adam taught Daniel the doggy paddle technique of swimming. Daniel was a quick learner and was soon swimming with little fear on his own.

By noon, the pool was completely packed with swimmers which did not deter the boys from their efforts to stay cool and have fun. There were many kids about their age, so the two quickly made friends. They learned the game "Marco Polo" from some of the kids they met and spent the entire afternoon chasing one another in the pool. It was around three-thirty when they finally got out of the pool and changed into dry clothing. Both boys were exhausted and waterlogged when they walked through the woods toward the path that would take them down the mountain. The tall trees lining the path provided them with shade from the sun, and a cool breeze was blowing in their face, and they made their way home.

"It's Saturday, so my dad usually gets pizza for dinner," Adam advised his friend.

Daniel had forgotten how hungry he was and thought that pizza would be the perfect thing to eat for dinner. It was around five when the boys got back to the Brodziak house. True to his word, four large boxes of pizza greeted them on the kitchen table, and the aroma of freshly baked pizza was too much for Daniel to bear. So when Mr. Brodziak invited them to dig in, Daniel felt no compunctions and began to help himself. It was the best pizza he had ever eaten. With his belly full and exhausted from a long day in the sun and water, Daniel had no problem falling quickly to sleep, grateful for his adoptive family and the kindness they were showing his family.

*****

"We're going to take a ride up to the Thiele mansion," Adam told his mother one morning. The Thiele Body Company was one of the oldest non-mining industries in Windber. It was established over a hundred years ago by W. J. Thiele, who manufactured horse-drawn wagons of various types. Now the plant was a major manufacturer of dump truck bodies. The Thieles had built a huge mansion on top of a mountain that overlooked the Town of Winder and the valley below. The Thiele plant was located at the foot of the mountain. Located next to the mansion was a horse farm where the Thieles bred thoroughbred racehorses.

Adam loved to see the horses and often rode his bike up the steep mountain to give the grazing horses carrots, apples, and sugar cubes. Even though he was only nine years old, Adam was already dreaming of becoming a horse veterinarian. He also wanted to own his own horse farm when he got bigger. To Adam, there was nothing more beautiful and splendid than a thoroughbred horse.

Adam's mother looked at him, wondering how he managed to have the energy to make the long ride from their home to the mansion. She never asked him any questions, however, as he always managed to find his way back home with no problems. But now he planned to drag Daniel with him.

"Does Daniel really want to ride a bike that far?" his mother asked.

"He'll be okay. He can use my old bike. We'll go slow."

Pauline Pryzinski had stopped worrying about her son and was surprised how much he had grown since they first got to Winder. It had only been a few weeks since they first got there, but he had already done things he would never have the opportunity to do back in Pittsburgh. "Let me pack you boys some lunch, and remember to bring your canteens and drink plenty of water. I'm also giving you some money so you can stop by at the Valley Dairy for some ice cream."

The Valley Dairy was an ice-cream making plant that had an ice-cream store attached which was on their way home from their bike ride. "Thanks, Mom. That would be great," Adam said, thinking of his favorite ice cream, cherry and vanilla.

The boys each carried backpacks and the boys' scout canteens were full of water. "Where is this mansion?" Daniel asked.

Adam looked at his friend and pointed in the direction of where they were going. Daniel looked up and could see the mansion perched high on the mountain in the distance. Even from where they were standing, the mansion could be seen clearly with its beautiful façade. "It looks like the White House where the president lives," Daniel commented has he mounted his bike for the long ride.

Before they had left, Adam took the last of the carrots and apples that his mother had stored in the cold cellar. He also packed a box of sugar cubes his father used to sweeten his coffee in the morning. Without saying a word, Adam began to pedal his bike down the hill. Daniel followed closely behind. They would ride their bikes down Graham Avenue and up the hill until they reached the small village of Rummel on the outskirts of Windber. From there, the cyclists turned right onto Hayes Street until intersected it with Route 56.

On the other side of Route 56, Hayes Street changed names to Statler Road. From here, the boys could see the entrance to the Thiele manufacturing plant on the left as they began to pedal forward. Statler Road was a steep road that led up the mountain for about a mile before coming to a dead end. Although the climb was hard, the boys only had to stop once to catch their breaths and to get a drink of water. At the top, the road opened up to reveal the horse farm with its beautiful white barn and white fences. Beyond the farmhouse was the Thiele mansion, more spectacular than Daniel had envisioned looking at it from afar. The boys pulled their bikes off the road and laid them on the ground near the fence. They could hear the neighing and snickering of horses as they climbed the fence to take a look.

There were at least fifty horses grazing in the pasture, most of which were mares with their foals they had given birth to in the spring. Adam whistled, wanting to gain the horses' attention. The response was immediate. Soon the boys were surrounded by several mares and their youngsters who came looking for treats. Adam quickly opened his backpack and retrieved the carrots, apples, and sugar. "Here, just reach out and wait for them to come to you. Don't be frightened. They love when I bring them treats."

Before he knew it, Daniel was feeding the horses. Although they were much bigger than he, Daniel did not feel any concern for his safety as he quickly learned how gentle these giants were. While they were feeding the horses, the boys could hear dogs barking in the background. This, Adam had learned from previous experience, was their cue to get going. The dogs were very protective of the horses and didn't take kindly to strangers. "Time to go," he said as he mounted his bike. Daniel followed him as they left their new friends behind.

The ride down the hill was much easier than it was going up as the bikers sped along with gravity pulling them faster and faster down the mountain. Within minutes, the boys were at the foot of the hill. They retraced their path up Hayes. Soon after they made a left turn onto Graham Avenue, the boys came to the Valley Dairy Ice-Cream Store. The small store was located in front of the ice-cream plant. The plant and store were founded back in 1938 and was another Windber landmark. The store provided the boys with a cool air-conditioned place to rest after their long ride. As they sat down on the stools located at the counter, they both realized how tired and hungry they were. Eating some ice cream right now would be the perfect answer.

"I always get vanilla with cherries ice cream. They call it White House ice cream, I guess because George Washington had cut down a cherry tree. I'm still not sure, but I love it," Adam told his friend. Daniel examined the ice-cream menu and decided on getting Strawberry ice cream. He loved strawberries.

After making a quick order of their ice-cream cone treats, they got back on their bikes. Now energized, they rode the rest of the way back to the Brodziak home and arrived exhausted but happy. As Daniel's mother helped him to remove his backpack, she gave her son a kiss and asked, "Did you boys have fun on your bike ride?"

She didn't have to wait for a response. She could tell from the look on her young son's face that he had a good day.

The two friends stayed busy the rest of the summer. If they weren't playing baseball, they would hike to the park to swim. Although they never rode their bikes back up to the horse farm again that summer, they would still ride their bikes all over town. Adam even took his friend on a hike to the Windber reservoir. The reservoir was located about five miles outside of town and was the main source of water for the town on Windber. With each adventure, the boys' friendship grew stronger and stronger. Daniel was not looking forward to going back to Pittsburgh but knew that day would soon be coming. Life in the small town of Windber during the summer of 1960 would be something that Daniel would remember and cherish for the rest of his life.

Chapter 27

Path to Recovery

Peter got into the back seat of the Buick that the Somerset County Alcohol Rehabilitation had sent to pick him up and looked out the rear window as the car drove away. He waved goodbye to his family who stood on the sidewalk in front of his house but was unsure if they could see him. Once they were out of sight, he turned to speak with his driver. "My name is Peter Pryzinski, what's yours," Peter asked, wanting to strike up a conversation.

"My name is Rodger," the driver responded.

Without waiting for any other response, Peter immediately began asking questions. Although he had agreed to admit himself into the rehab center, he still was unclear as to what to expect. "Have you been working long at the rehab center? How long will it take to get there? Are there many other people who are staying at the center?" Peter continued his barrage of questions without giving Rodger time to respond. Finally, during a break in the questioning, Rodger began answering some of Peter's questions as best he could remember them.

Rodger had been working at the rehab center for over ten years. He was at one time a client who had gotten sober after spending several years off and on at the center. He went on to say that he's been sober now for over ten years. "You're going to love it there," Rodger said encouragingly to Peter. "The staff there is great, and you'll get to meet other guys who are dealing with the same problems you are."

Before Peter knew it, the car was entering the ramp to the Pennsylvania Turnpike, and according to the sign, they were driving east toward Harrisburg. "It's only an hour's drive from here. We'll get off the Somerset exit, and the rehab center is only a short drive from there."

Suddenly Peter realized that all this was real. There would be no turning back now. He had agreed to get help with his drinking problem and to go to the rehab center to get it. He was now determined to carry it out and keep his promise to his wife. He only hoped that it wouldn't take him years as it did Rodger.

*****

Pauline met Dr. Slevic at his office in Windber shortly after she arrived. She still had not obtained permission to visit her husband in person and was becoming concerned about the delay. She didn't want Peter to feel abandoned, even though she knew that he was aware of the visitation restrictions. Dr. Tom took the opportunity to explain what was going to happen to Peter while he was staying at the rehabilitation center.

Pauline learned that the first step in any treatment program for alcoholism was to withdraw from alcohol. This is often the most difficult part of rehab physically because withdrawal from alcohol can create uncomfortable and even dangerous, physical, and psychological symptoms. After having finished detoxing, Peter will continue on with his recovery work. He would receive various types of behavioral therapies which would include cognitive-behavioral therapy, contingency management, and motivational-enhancement therapy. Dr. Tom went on to provide Pauline with more details about each of these therapies.

Toward the end of his stay, there would also be a family therapy session which allowed a client to improve familial relationships while helping everyone learn to practice healthier behaviors that are supportive of recovery. Pauline listened intently and was grateful for the education, but all she wanted to know was when she would be able to see her husband.

"I've pulled some strings and got the center's permission to allow you to visit Peter every Saturday morning as long as he continues to show progress with his rehabilitation," Slevic informed her.

"Saturday... That's tomorrow!" Pauline exclaimed as she got up and hugged the doctor. "I can't begin to thank you for all of the help you've given my husband and my family."

"Don't thank me just yet. Peter is the one who has to do all the work. His recovery will depend on how motivated he is to get sober," the doctor warned.

*****

Pauline got up early on Saturday morning. Although the drive from Windber to Somerset would take less than an hour, Pauline was anxious to see her husband and to get on the road early. Kathryn had agreed to drive Pauline to the rehabilitation center since she knew the best way to get there. After saying their goodbyes to Ben and the boys, the two women started their journey to Somerset, Pennsylvania.

Being alone in the car together gave them time to talk for the first time since Pauline had arrived in Windber. "I really appreciate all the help you've given us and for letting Daniel and me stay at your home. I don't know what we would have done without you guys. Peter's been a mess for such a long time, and I'm not sure that he would have agreed to go into rehab if it weren't for you and your husband and Dr. Slevic and Ann. Peter is really a good person, and I want him back the way he used to be before he started drinking. I really love my husband, and I'll do whatever it takes to get him well."

Kathryn looked at her friend and reached down to grab her hand. "I can't say that I know what you're going through, but I know it can't be easy. You and Daniel can stay with us as long as you want. If you hadn't noticed, Daniel and Adam are becoming good friends. Meeting one another has been the best thing for both boys."

Pauline nodded her head. She had left so quickly this morning that she didn't have much to talk to her son. "I wonder what they have planned today," she said.

"Adam is going to take Daniel swimming today up at the park. He wants to show Daniel a secret path he claims to have found through the woods near the park. It is about a two-mile hike from our house to the park, so the boys should be good and tired by the time they get home. Ben's picking up pizza, so we don't have to worry about making dinner tonight."

Pauline felt a little embarrassed that she did not know what plans her son had made. "That sounds like fun. I've been so preoccupied with Peter that I've kind of ignored my own son. I didn't know he was planning to go swimming today. He doesn't even know how to swim. I didn't even pack him a bathing suit."

"Don't worry," Pauline responded, "Daniel borrowed one of Adam's swimsuits, and I gave each one a towel to dry off with. Adam is a good swimmer, and he'll watch out for Daniel. I'm sure that they will have fun." Little did Pauline realize how much this new relationship with the Brodziak family would affect both her husband and her son.

On the outskirts of Windber, Kathryn turned south on Route 160 until it intersected at a crossroads. She then turned left at the crossroads toward the little village of Central City. From there, she planned to catch Route 30 and drive west toward Somerset. It was a beautiful, clear day, and the trip took them past several large dairy farms. Pauline could see the herds of cows grazing in the pasture as they drove past the farms. These were things she would never see living in Pittsburgh.

"I wonder how Peter is doing today. Do you think he'll be glad to see me?" Pauline asked more to herself than to Kathryn.

"Of course, he will, why wouldn't he?" Kathryn responded.

"I guess I just don't know what to expect. It hasn't been easy living with him these past years, but we've never been apart for this long. I didn't realize just how much I missed him. All I want is for him to get well and to be able to come home soon. I really do love the man very much, and I know that the boys miss him as well."

Pauline stopped as she felt tears begin to well up in her eyes. Sensing her anxiety, Kathryn tried to console her friend. "You just need to be strong for both you and your family. Let's pray to God that he gives Peter the strength and determination to get sober. From what little I've seen of the man, it seems that he loves you guys very much and will do whatever it takes to get well."

The trip to Somerset took longer than expected, but soon they arrived at the rehab center. The Somerset County Alcohol and Drug Rehabilitation Center was located on a sprawling thirty-acre campus located five miles north of the Somerset. Pauline was immediately impressed by the serenity of the facility and the beauty of the campus itself. "Wow, I wasn't expecting this," she said as Kathryn pulled up and parked the car near the front entrance to the main building.

"I can't go in, so I'll just wait for you here in the car," Kathryn announced as she turned off the ignition.

Dr. Slevic had made it clear that Pauline was the only one who could see Peter, at least during this first-time visit. "Okay, wish me luck and say some prayers," Pauline said as she exited the car.

Before entering the building, Pauline turned and waved to Kathryn as she was sitting in the car. She tried to shake off the apprehension she felt as she opened the door.

"I'm here to see Peter Pryzinski," she said to the receptionist who greeted her.

"Do you have an appointment?" Pauline's anxiety heighted at hearing this question. She wasn't sure if she had an appointment. "Dr. Slevic had made arrangements for me to see my husband," she finally responded.

"Okay, the doctor is in today, so I'll check with him first. Have a seat." The doctor never told her that he would be working today, Pauline thought as she took a seat in a nearby chair. *I hope everything is okay.*

Shortly afterward, Dr. Slevic appeared and greeted Pauline. "Welcome to our recovery center. How was your drive here? I hope you found us okay," the doctor said in a matter-of-fact tone.

"Kathryn Brodziak drove me here today. She knew exactly where she was going, so there was no problem. When can I see my husband?" Pauline demanded, wanting to forgo any further conversation.

"He's finishing up with one of our behavioral therapy sessions right now and will be down to see you shortly," the doctor explained.

"I've reserved a meeting room here on the first floor where you can talk with him in private. I'll take you there." With that, the two got up and walked through the same door from which the doctor had first come through. The floor contained a number of rooms that reminded her of her college classrooms.

They entered one of the rooms which contained a table surrounded by chairs. "Before Peter gets here, I wanted to talk with you first, Pauline. Your husband has made some significant progress since he first got here, but he still has a long way to go. Has Peter every spoken to you much about what his World War II experience in the Navy?"

The question took Pauline off guard, causing her to stop and think. "Come to think about it, Doctor, I don't think he's ever talked to me about it. Why? Is that important?"

Dr. Tom looked her in the eyes before answering, "The medical profession is starting to see a significant amount of World War II veterans who are having drinking problems. Since he's been here, that's all Peter wants to talk about to our therapists. It's like he's been holding it in for all these years and now feels free to let everything out. Peter saw some very horrible things while he was fighting in the war, and we feel that what he witnessed subconsciously caused him so much pain that he could only drown it out with alcohol. For some reason, these veterans never want to talk about it, which is the worst thing they can do. Half of our clients here at the center are veterans who are having the same problem as Peter, some even much worse.

"Peter will need to continue with both psychological and behavioral therapy probably for the rest of his life. He's a strong-willed man who has shown us his willingness to overcome his drinking problem. He will need your support once he leaves here if he plans to stay sober. He will have to attend weekly psychological counseling sessions. He will also benefit from attending weekly Alcoholics Anonymous meetings in the Pittsburgh area. Before he leaves this facility to go home, we'll assign him a mentor that he can reach out and talk to whenever he feels it would be helpful.

"I know that this is a lot for you to take in, but I think it's important to know why your husband started to drink in the first place. I imagine that you may have been blaming yourself all these years, but you shouldn't. There is a medical reason he started to drink, and I think that we can cure him."

Just then, the door to the meeting room opened. Peter stood there, looking at his wife. She immediately got up and ran to him, throwing her arms around him, crying. "Peter, I love you so much," she said over and over as she kissed him nonstop. The two held one another for a long time. "You going to be okay, sweetheart. Get well so you can come home soon," Pauline said as she released her hold of him. For the first time in years, she felt a sense of hope. Thanks to the support of her newfound friends and for God's help, her husband was finally on the path to recovery.

Chapter 28

The Pennant

After spending over thirty days in the Alcohol Recovery Center Peter was ready to go home to Pittsburgh. Although his recovery had been slow, he felt that he had made significant progress and was now ready to go it alone. After her initial visit, Pauline was able to visit Peter every weekend and was permitted to stay longer and longer with each follow-up visit. Toward the end of Peter's stay, both Pauline and Daniel were able to visit him every day and were even given the opportunity to participate in several family counseling sessions. With every visit, Pauline's confidence level in her husband's recovery increased, and she expressed her hope and gratitude to Dr. Slevic and the staff for all of their help.

But now it was time to get on with their lives and return to their home in Pittsburgh, so on one bright sunny day toward the end of August, Pauline and Daniel said their goodbyes to the Brodziak family and their summer home in Windber and drove to Somerset to pick up Peter. Daniel and Adam had been inseparable during their visit, so saying farewell was difficult for the boys. As they were saying their goodbyes, they first shook hands, then hugged one another. "Thanks for all the good times. I'll never forget this place or you. I'm not sure when the next we'll get to see one another, but try to keep in touch.," Daniel said to Adam as he got into the back seat of his mother's car.

"Keep rooting those Bucco's on," Adam said as he waved to his friend. Little did the boys know at the time, but they would meet again sooner than either could have ever expected and under the most incredible circumstances that both would remember for the rest of their lives.

Although his mother had called his brothers almost every day since they left Pittsburgh over a month ago, his mother gave Daniel little opportunity to speak with them. The telephone calls to Pittsburgh were long distance and she did not want to make the phone calls to her sons longer than necessary in hope of keeping the long-distance charges down. Letting Daniel speak would only prolong the calls longer than need be. She offered to pay for the telephone bills, but the Brodziak's refused to accept any reimbursement from Pauline. So when Daniel finally got home from his extended visit to Windber, his brothers greeted him with open arms and hugs.

"Looks like you grew three inches since we last saw you, brother," Michael said as he playfully rubbed his brother's head. "Believe it or not, but we missed you, brother. Welcome home."

The truth was that Daniel did get taller and heavier while he was away and in fact grew more than three inches and was ten pounds heavier. "It's good to be home," Daniel halfheartedly replied. Although he was glad to be back home, he realized that he was once again the youngest of the Pryzinski boys, which made him the lowest man on the totem pole. It would take him a while to readjust to his new way of life, but during his absence, he had gained a sense of confidence and maturity he did not have when he first left home. His older brothers felt the maturity change in their brother and could see firsthand the physical change in him, so they began to treat Daniel with more respect and more as a peer and less as their youngest brother. Besides, he had grown so big that he was now bigger than his middle brother, Luke, and was quickly catching up to Michael.

It was now September 2, 1960, and Daniel would be going back to school in a week. The Pirates had just beaten the San Francisco Giants the night before, 6 to 1, which gave them a commanding seven game lead over the Milwaukee Braves in the National League pennant race. During his stay in Windber, he and Adam tried to

406

listen to as many Pirates games as possible, but they were usually too tired at the end of the day to listen to night games. The Pirates had just returned from a successful road trip to the west coast, where they had dominated both the Dodgers and the Giants. Due to the difference in time, it was impossible for the boys to listen to any of those games and had to rely mainly on newspaper reports of the games the next day.

Now that he was back home in Pittsburgh, and without any distractions, Daniel was now ready to focus his full attention on the remaining Pirates game. Pirates fever was beginning to take hold in the City of Pittsburgh as mostly everyone began to realize that the Pirates had a legitimate chance to win the National League Pennant, which would be their first in thirty-three years. There were only twenty-seven games left to play in the 1960 baseball season. The Pirates currently maintained a 79-win and a 49-loss record. This was also the best record in the Major League, followed closely by the mighty New York Yankees whose record was 75–50. If things stayed as they were, the Pirates would be playing the Yankees for the World Series Championship, something that Daniel was not looking forward to. Of all the teams to play, why would it have to be the Yankees? Their star-studded line-up included such baseball stars as Yogi Berra, Mickey Mantle, Roger Maris, Whitely Ford, and Tony Kubek. The Yankees were a team well accustomed to the stress of playing in a World Series and had won six championships over the past ten years going back to 1950, including the last one in 1958 when they defeated the Milwaukee Braves in seven games. The Pirates appeared to be no match for this powerhouse baseball team. First things first, however, the Pirates needed to win the pennant. With twenty-seven games left, anything could happen.

KDKA was the local Pittsburgh radio and TV station that broadcasted the Pittsburgh Pirates baseball games in 1960. The station began to run contests, offering various types of prizes to anyone who could guess the date on which the Pirates would clinch the pennant. A contestant not only had to guess the date but also the score of the game on that date. This made the contest one that was difficult to win. Regardless, thousands of fans would enter their names along with their guesses each date by going to local department stores throughout the Pittsburgh area where boxes were set up to deposit a fan's entry. This added additional excitement to the final weeks of the season as Pirate fans stayed tuned to each game, trying to guess the magic date that they would clinch the pennant.

The Pirates would go on to win the pennant on Sunday, September 25, 1960. On that date, the Pirates lost to the Milwaukee Braves, 4 to 2 in 10 innings; however, at the same time on that date, the Cardinals lost to the Chicago Cubs, 5–0. The combined results of both games enabled the Pirates to clinch the pennant. The City of Pittsburgh went crazy after learning that their beloved team had won the National League Pennant and would be playing in the World Series. The game with the Braves had been played in Milwaukee, so the city had to wait until the next day to greet their heroes and to celebrate their accomplishment.

A huge crowd had gathered at Pittsburgh airport and was there when the team got off the airplane after their flight from Milwaukee. All of the Pittsburgh TV stations, including KDKA, were on hand to televise the teams return home. Daniel had listened to the Brave's game on the radio and was disappointed that they lost, but his hero, Bill Mazeroski, had hit a solo home run, his eleventh of the year, to break a scoreless tie. Bill had improved his batting average by twenty points since the beginning of the year and was getting hot toward the end of the season, just in time for the World Series. The next time the Pirates would play would be a home game against the Cincinnati Reds on Tuesday, September 27. The game was a near sellout with over twenty-two thousand fans in attendance to greet their 1960 National League Champions.

To their delight, the Pirates won in 16 innings, 4–3. Even though it was a school night, Daniel's parents allowed him to stay up late to listen to the entire game. The 1960 regular season for the Pittsburgh Pirates came to an end on October 2 with the Pirates winning the last game, 9–5, against their rivals, the Milwaukee Braves. The Pirates ended the regular season with a 95–59 record and would now be moving on to play the New York Yankees, who had finished their season with a 97–57 record in the 1960 World Series.

The City of Pittsburgh was overwhelmed with excitement, and the expectations of playing in a World Series drove the fans to near hysteria. It didn't matter that the Pirates would be a decided underdog to win the championship against the Yankees. Their beloved Buccos had made it after playing a magical regular season, where they had led the National League almost the entire way. KDKA decided to run a new contest which was the most exciting of all. As luck would have it, the National League team would be the home team for the 1960 World Series. This meant that four of the seven games would be played at Forbes Field.

To celebrate their championship and to reward the fans for their loyalty, the Pirates and KDKA would be chancing off four free tickets to each of the four home games. In order to participate in the contest, all a fan needed to do was to visit the station in Pittsburgh and fill out a form with their name, address, and phone number. The contest was the buzz of the town, and the response from the fans was immediate and overwhelming to the point that the station offered to keep their doors open for twenty-four hours in response to the demand.

After first hearing about the contest, Daniel immediately asked his father if he could go to the station to register for the contest. "Please, Dad?" Daniel begged. "This may be the last time we'll ever be able to see a World Series game."

Peter looked at his son with some skepticism. He knew that the odds of winning such a contest must be a million to one, but he didn't want to disappoint his youngest son. "Okay, son, tomorrow after school, you and I will take the bus downtown and enter for the contest." Although it had been almost a month since his discharge from the rehab center, Peter still had not returned to work at the steel mill. Since returning home, Peter maintained weekly meetings with a local counselor he met from contacts he had at the clinic. He was also attending weekly Alcoholics Anonymous meetings with a group of men in the Pittsburgh area who were also suffering from alcohol abuse. He was also assigned a mentor who lived in the Polish Hill area, who Peter kept in touch with on a daily basis.

Peter had also decided to go back to church, so in addition to attending Sunday Mass, he also went to eight o'clock mass every morning. The spiritual support he received from his daily prayers at Mass was just as important to him as the support he was receiving from the external support groups. Thanks to all of this support, Peter was able to continue to stay sober. He had not had a drink since the day he attended the Pirates' doubleheader back in July. He still was not ready to go back to work, however, and since he was still receiving disability payments from his union, Peter decided to stay home a little longer. So this gave him the opportunity to spend more time with his family. Taking Daniel on a bus ride downtown was an opportune time for him to get reacquainted with his baseball-loving son.

*****

The next afternoon, after Daniel got home from school, the two took the local bus downtown to the KDKA station in Pittsburgh. This was the first time that Daniel was able to spend time alone with his father in a very long time. During the bus ride, the two talked nonstop about a lot of things that young boys talk about with their fathers but mostly about baseball and the Pittsburgh Pirates. He also spoke about his stay in Windber and the friendship he had made with Adam Brodziak. Peter never knew that his son was such a talker, and he made up his mind that he would make every effort to set aside time in his life to speak with all his sons, especially his youngest boy, who probably needed his guidance more than ever. His recovery from alcoholism would be meaningless unless his family benefited from his sobriety.

The bus ride downtown took about thirty minutes. As he and his father exited the bus, Daniel marveled at the sight of the tall building that enveloped the downtown Pittsburgh landscape. They walked several blocks to the Gateway Center which served as the headquarters for KDKA radio and TV. Back in 1956, KDKA had relocated its studios from the Grant Building to Gateway Center, joining KDKA-TV. The Gateway Center is a complex of office, residential, and hotel buildings covering twenty-five acres in Downtown Pittsburgh. The KDKA logo greeted them as they walked into the front lobby of the station. To their surprise, there weren't many people in the lobby. They were immediately greeted by a receptionist seated behind a desk.

"I want to enter my name for the Pirates World Series tickets," Peter said without knowing exactly what he had to do.

The receptionist smiled at him and handed him a sheet of paper. "Here, fill out this entry form, and give it back to me," the receptionist instructed. "You can use the desk over there in the corner."

Peter took the entry form and walked to the desk where he found a pen. The entry form was simple. All he did was to provide his name, address, and telephone number and sign the form confirming that he was twenty-one years of age. The form contained the rules and regulations for anyone entering the contest. In addition to being twenty-one years of age, the contestant would have to agree to wear a KDKA T-shirt at the game, which would identify him or her as the contest winner.

The winner would receive four tickets to any one of the four home games being played at Forbes Field during the 1960 World Series. Transportation to the game was not included. The World Series was scheduled to begin on Wednesday, October 5, 1960, with a home game at Forbes Field. The other three home games would be played on October 6, October 12, and October 13. The winners of the contest were to be announced on Tuesday, October 4, at twelve noon on a radio broadcast from KDKA. After completing the form, Peter returned it to the receptionist.

"Good luck," she said. "Hope you win. Don't forget to listen to the radio on Tuesday to find out who wins the tickets."

Peter turned and grabbed his son's hand. "Let's go, Daniel. Your mom will have dinner waiting for us when we get home." Although the odds of winning these World Series tickets were slim to none, Peter felt a great amount of satisfaction that he was giving his son hope that he would be able to see his beloved Pirates play in the World Series.

School throughout the City of Pittsburgh was cancelled on October 5 and 6 in anticipation of seeing the first two games of the World Series. Unfortunately for Daniel, he still had to go to school on

Tuesday the 4th, the day the contest winners would be announced. Although he was not normally allowed to leave the school grounds during lunch, Daniel had decided to run home to listen to the KDKA broadcast. So when the noon lunch bell rang, Daniel was the first out the door and ran the three blocks to his home. His dad was sitting by the radio as he ran into the house, out of breath and sweating. "Have they announced the contest winner yet, Dad?"

"Not yet.," his father replied. "You got here just in time. Come sit down." The station was playing a commercial for Iron City Beer followed by another for some detergent Daniel had never heard of. Finally, a voice on the other end announced, "Okay, Pirate fans, are you ready to find out which lucky ones will be going to see the Pirates and Yankees play in the World Series? We'll pick the winning entry form one at a time and announce each winner. For the October 5th game, the winner is…"

One by one, each winner was announced, until only the last home game, the seventh game of the 1960 World Series scheduled for October 13 was announced. "And the last winner is Peter Pryzinski of Pittsburgh, Pennsylvania. You and three guests will be going to the seventh game of the World Series complements of KDKA Radio and TV. Congratulations to all of our winners!"

Both Daniel and his dad sat in the living room, shocked by the announcement they had just heard. Never in his wildest imagination did Peter think they would win. His son, on the other hand, was screaming at the top of his lungs, "I knew we would win! I knew we would win!" Daniel kept saying it over and over again.

"Okay, son, just calm down. You need to get back to school. You can tell everyone that we're going to see the Pirates play in the World Series."

Daniel immediately got up and ran to the front door. He couldn't wait to tell everyone. He stopped short just before leaving and turned unexpectedly to his father. "Dad, I want to invite Adam and his father to go to this game with us. Would that be, okay?"

Peter did not know what to say. He had two other boys who would like nothing more than to go see a World Series game. "What about your brothers? Don't you think they would like to go?"

Daniel looked at his father. "Adam is my best friend, Dad. He and his family were so nice to us during our visit. I know that my brothers would understand."

"Let's talk more about it tonight when you get home from school. If your brothers agree to it, I have no problem in asking the Brodziaks to go with us." Peter knew that would be a tall order, but he agreed in the back of his mind that letting Adam and Ben go with them to the game would be a nice way to repay them for all of their kindness over the past summer. Besides, without the help he received from them, he may not be sober today.

There was one other small detail that Peter did not want to share with Daniel just then during all the excitement. The Pirates were a decided underdog in the 1960 World Series. Many baseball experts outside of Pittsburgh were picking the mighty Yankees to sweep the Pirates in four straight games. If that happened, there would be no seventh game at home on October 13. Another contest rule that Peter did not share with Daniel was that winning tickets for the last two home games was contingent upon the Pirates being able to get that far. Little did Peter know at the time, but the 1960 World Series would not only go to the seventh game, but that the Series and especially the seventh game would be filled with miracles that no baseball expert could have ever predicted.

Chapter 29

The World Series

Next to Pauline Pryzinski, her son, Michael, had been most affected by his father's seemly miraculous recovery from his drinking problem. As the oldest son, Michael had been closer to his father than his younger brothers and was the one who best remembered the good days before his dad started to drink. Michael had always admired his father and looked upon him as more like a best friend. So he was devastated beyond reason when his father first started to drink. To him, the metamorphosis from being a loving father and husband to an argumentative and verbally abusive drunk was too much for him to handle. He soon became withdrawn and stopped eating to the point of becoming anorexic. It was his way of releasing his frustrations and to protest against his father for the way he had become.

At one point, he contemplated running away from home, but where would he go? He felt helpless and alone. It took Michael over a year before he realized that these protests were achieving no results other than making him feel sick and emaciated. He had lost over twenty pounds during that first year, but neither of his parents seemed to notice or even care (at least that's how he felt). He didn't want to blame his mother because she had her hands full, trying to keep the family together while dealing with his father's daily alcohol-induced tirades. Michael resigned himself to the fact that his dad would never be the same and that there was nothing he or anyone else could do to save him.

So when Michael began to see the changes in his father after returning home from his stay in the alcohol rehab center, he became cautiously optimistic. He had also begun to feel a great deal of affinity and gratitude toward the Brodziak family. Although he never got to know them well, Michael gave them full credit for helping his father and would forever be indebted to them for what they did. So when his father approached him and his brother Luke about offering the World Series tickets he had just won to Adam and Ben Brodziak, Michael was the first to agree to the idea. "Dad, whatever you feel is the best," Michael responded. "We owe those folks a great deal of gratitude, and I, for one, have no problems with you giving them the tickets."

Luke was not much of a baseball fan, so he quickly agreed as well.

"I'm proud of you, boys. That's very generous of both of you, and I won't forget it. Ben and Adam are good people, and I'd like to do something for them to thank them for all of their kindness and help."

Later on that evening, Peter called and spoke with Ben Brodziak. It was just then that he realized that he hadn't spoken to Ben since that day back in July when the folks from Windber all intervened on his behalf to convince him to seek help with his drinking problem. Peter never had the chance to thank him or Ben's wife for all of their help and kindness.

"Ben, this is Peter Pryzinski. I hope you remember me," Peter said sheepishly.

"Peter, it's great to hear from you! How's everything going? We miss you guys," Ben responded.

It took a second for Peter to reply. "Listen, Ben I never had a chance to thank you and Kathryn for all of your help. Thanks to you folks, I feel that my life has finally turned around. I've been sober ever since the last time we met back in July. I can't thank you enough."

"Don't give it a second thought, Peter, that's what friends are for. We loved having Pauline and Daniel stay with us this past summer. My son talks about Daniel every day, and I know he misses him."

"That's why I'm calling you, Ben," Peter replied. "You're not going to believe it, Ben, but we've just won four tickets to the seventh game of the World Series!" Peter went on to explain to Ben the events that led up to him winning the tickets. "Daniel and I would like to invite you and Adam to come to the game with us, providing that the Pirates make it to game seven."

"Wow, that's an amazing story. Sure, we'd love to go with you guys to the game!" Ben responded without hesitation. "Adam, guess what? We're going to see the Pirates play in the World Series!" Ben yelled excitedly to his son who was standing close by.

"Just remember, Ben, that it's going to all depend on whether or not there will be a game seven, so please do not get too excited just yet," Peter warned.

The two men went on to make plans should there be a seventh game. It was decided that Ben and Adam would drive to Pittsburgh the day before and stay at the Pryzinski house. The foursome would wake up early and catch a bus that would take them to Forbes Field. After hanging up with Ben, Peter sat down on the sofa next to his wife. "They've accepted our invitation," he told Pauline.

"I'll go upstairs to let Daniel know. He'll be so excited."

As he stood, Peter felt a little dizzy. He sat back down to regain his composure. At the same time, Peter felt a slight pain in his chest but thought nothing of it. He had been experiencing this pain for over a week and attributed it to indigestion, nothing more. "Are you okay, sweetheart?" Pauline asked. "Sit down and rest. Daniel can wait to hear the news."

She was right. The pain in his chest was going away, as was his dizziness. He looked at his wife and smiled. He must be the luckiest guy in the world. He had a beautiful wife and children and wonderful friends who cared for him. "Thank you, God. I know that I probably don't deserve it, but thank you for everything you've given me in my life," Peter prayed silently to himself.

*****

Forbes Field was built in 1909 and was constructed on the edge of Schenley Park in the Oakland Section of Pittsburgh, Pennsylvania, near the campus of the University of Pittsburgh. The spacious outfield overlooked the Schenley Park, and in October of 1960, the leaves on the trees in the park were turning bright orange, yellow, and red, marking the beginning of the fall season and adding a picturesque view for those fans attending the World Series. The Cathedral of Learning is a forty-two-story skyscraper that serves as the centerpiece of the University of Pittsburgh's main campus in the Oakland neighborhood and stands as a sentinel overlooking left field that can be seen from almost anywhere inside Forbes Field. So the scene that greeted the New York Yankees as they took the field in Pittsburgh for game 1 of the 1960 World Series was one that was a far cry from their busy home field in the Bronx section of New York City.

In addition, Pittsburgh was just a small almost Midwestern type of city with a population of about 500,000 which was dwarfed by the City of New York with its population of over 7 million. Their baseball fields were built accordingly, with Forbes Field seating 36,600 while Yankee stadium seats 70,000. The series was portrayed as a modern-day David versus Goliath by most baseball news media of the day.

Game 1 of the 1960 World Series was played on Wednesday, October 5, 1960. The Pirates would be starting their pitching ace, Vern Law, while the Yankees opened the series with pitcher Art Ditmar. After erasing the lead off Yankee runner by a double play, New York Yankees right fielder, Roger Maris, opened up the scoring with a home run to right field that gave the Yankees the early lead 1–0. The Pirates scored three runs in the bottom of the first thanks to a walk of Bill Virdon and double by Dick Groat and a single by Roberto Clemente. Ditmars only pitched a one-third inning and was quickly replaced by Jim Coates, so at the end of the inning, the Pirates were winning 3–1. The underdog Pirates would go on to win game 1, 6–4. Law pitched 7 innings and gave up only 2 earned runs. Elroy Face pitched the last two innings and earned the save. The game also featured a home run by Bill Mazeroski, who went 2 for 4 and had 2 runs batted in. At the end of the game, the sellout crowd of 36,676 went wild. Most baseball experts had predicted their team to get swept by the mighty Yankees, but this opening series win gave them hope that maybe the Pirates could win the World Series.

The Pirate faithful's hopes was short-lived, however, because on the very next day, October 6, 1960, the revenge-driven Yankees returned to Forbes Field and destroyed the Pirates by a score of 16–3. The Bombers accumulated 19 hits in the win, including 2 home runs by Micky Mantle. Yankees starter Bobby Turley pitched 8 1/3 inning and got the win. The Pirates had sent six pitchers to the mound, including starter Bob Friend, who got the loss. The series would now move from Pittsburgh to New York with the series tied 1–1.

Little would change for the upstart Pirates in game 3 as they faced the Yankees ace, Whitey Ford, who promptly shut out the Corsairs 10–0. The Yankees again outhit the Pirates 16 to 4 on their way to win the game and to take a series lead 2–1.

Vern Law was again back on the mound for game 4, and the results were decidedly different with the Pirates winning the away game versus the Yankees 3–2. The Yankees scored first in the bottom of the fourth inning and took an early 1–0 lead. The Pirates countered in the top of the fifth inning, scoring 3 runs helped in part by double to left filed by pitcher Vern Law. The Yankees could score only one more run against Law who pitched eight innings and got the win. Elroy Face came in in relief and earned another World Series save. The series was now tied 2–2 with one more game to be played in Yankee Stadium. This win guaranteed that the Pirates would be playing the last two games of the Series at home in Forbes Field.

Entering game 5 on October 10 at home in Yankee Stadium, few offered little if any hope that the Pirates would win. For the first time in the Series, the Pirates would be starting Harvey Haddix. The Yankees would be relying upon their opening day starter, Art Ditmar, to pitch game 5. Harvey Haddix was a scrappy left-handed pitcher who had earned an 11-win, 10 loss 1960 regular season pitching record with an ERA of 3.97. At age thirty-four, Harvey was also the oldest of the Pirates' starting pitchers. Back on May 26, 1959, Harvey had pitched a perfect game for twelve innings against the Milwaukee Braves but lost the game in a thirteenth inning. If only he could win game 5 in Yankee Stadium, the Pirates felt that it would give them a fighting chance to win the World Series.

The Pirates opened the scoring in the top of second by scoring 3 runs off of the Yankee starter Ditmar, thanks in part to a two run doubles by Bill Mazeroski. After that, the home team favorites could only muster 2 runs on only 5 hits. The Pirates shocked the baseball world by winning game 5 at Yankee Stadium 5–2. Haddix pitched 6 1/3 earnings to gain the win. Face again came in on relief and earned his third save of the series. Miraculously, the Pittsburgh Pirates had taken 2 games out 3 against the Yankees at home and would be returning to Forbes Field with a 3–2 series lead.

With the Pirates needing only one more win to take the 1960 World Series, the Yankees were taking no chances, so on Tuesday, October 12, 1960, the Yankees again sent Whitey Ford to the mound to pitch game number 6. The Pirates again countered with Bob Friend. Although Friend had a stellar 1960 season with a team second best pitching record on 18–12 and an ERA of 3.08, he would prove to be no match against Whitey Ford, who dominated game 6, giving up only 7 hits on his way to a 12–0 Yankees win. Friend had pitched poorly and was relieved after pitching only 2 innings, giving up 5 hits and 5 earned runs.

With the series now tied 3–3, the stage was now set for the seventh game of the World Series. The underdog Pirates had achieved more than was ever expected of them. The Pirates faithful now could only wait and pray that their team could only win one more game.

The telephone hanging on the wall of the Brodziak home rang and rang until finally, Kathryn Brodziak picked it up to answer. "Hello, can I speak with Adam?" the young voice asked on the other end of the connection.

"Who is this?" Kathryn asked.

"I'm sorry, Mrs. Brodziak. This is Daniel Pryzinski. Did you hear that the Pirates are going to play game seven of the World Series? That means we will all be going," Daniel said with an excited tone of voice.

"Yes, I know. We just finished watching the game. Hold on, dear, while I get Adam. I know he's just as excited as you are." Daniel held the line for what seemed like an eternity to him. Finally, Adam picked up the phone.

"Hi, Daniel. Looks like we're going to see one another again soon. I can't wait to see you again." Although he, too, was glad to be seeing his friend again, Daniel was more excited about being able to see a World Series game. "Can you believe this is happening! We're going to the World Series! The Pirates have a chance to win a World Series Championship!"

The boys continued their discussion for ten minutes before Daniel's father interrupted, "I need to speak with Adam's father, Daniel. You and Adam have been on the phone long enough."

"Okay, Dad. See you soon, Adam. I can't wait."

Each boy transferred the telephones to their fathers who then spent another ten minutes exchanging pleasantries and their excitement about going to see the Pirates and the Yankees play in game 7. Shortly after hanging up with Peter Pryzinski, Ben began to prepare for the two-hour drive to Pittsburgh. It was Tuesday, October 12. Game number 7 of the 1960 World Series was scheduled to be played at 1:00 p.m. the following day, Wednesday, October 13, so they had no time to waste. Ben had already packed a suitcase with clothes and had placed it in the trunk of his car, anticipating that he would have to drive to Pittsburgh. Ben and Adam said their goodbyes to the rest of the family, got into the family car, and began their journey to Pittsburgh. Neither knew what to expect, and little could they have ever imagined that in just a short twenty-four hours, they would be witnessing one of the greatest baseball games ever played. Little did they also know that the events that would take place on October 13, while attending the game, would also provide them all with challenges that would forever change their lives.

Chapter 30

Game 7

Going into game number 7 of the 1960 World Series, the New York Yankees had statistically dominated the series, outscoring the Pirates, 46 runs to 17 runs. The Yankees won three blowouts (16–3, 10–0, and 12–0), while the Pirates won three close games (6–4, 3–2, 5–2). The weather for all of the six games had been perfect. Wednesday, October 13, 1960, in Pittsburgh, Pennsylvania, was no exception as the teams exchanged their lineup cards to the umpires prior to the beginning of game 7. The Pirates would again be relying on pitcher Vern Law while the Yankees would be starting right-hander Bob Turley. The lineups and batting order for each team were as follows:

Yankees

   1 Bobby Richardson: 2B
   2 Tony Kubek: SS
   3 Roger Maris: RF
   4 Mickey Mantle: CF
   5 Yogi Berra: LF
   6 Bill Skowron: 1B
   7 Johnny Blanchard: C
   8 Clete Boyer: 3B
   9 Bob Turley: P

Pirates

1 Bill Virdon: CF
2 Dick Groat: SS
3 Bob Skinner: LF
4 Rocky Nelson: 1B
5 Roberto Clemente: RF
6 Smoky Burgess: C
7 Don Hoak: 3B
8 Bill Mazeroski: 2B
9 Vern Law: P

As they had planned, the four ticket winners had left the Pryzinski home in Polish Hill early, walked to the corner, and caught the bus that ran next to Forbes Field early and arrived before the gates opened at noon. Each was wearing the T-shirts that KDKA had given them, announcing them as the winners of the game 7 tickets. On the backs of the T-shirts were printed the Pirates logo along with the words, "Beat 'Em, Bucs," which had become the team's slogan during the 1960 regular seasons. So the foursome was treated somewhat like royalty by the ushers as they took their seats, which were located ten rows directly behind home plate. Neither the Pirates nor KDKA had spared any expense in providing the winners with the best seats in Forbes Field.

"Wow, I never expected this," Peter Pryzinski proclaimed as they took their seats. Ben, Adam, and Daniel were too excited and awestruck to say anything. "I didn't know we'd be so close to the field. You can see everything from here."

Shortly after exchanging the lineups, the sellout crowd of 36,683 fans were asked to stand for the playing of the National Anthem. The boys removed their baseball caps and proudly stood and sang "The Star-Spangled Banner." Afterward, they could hear the umpires yell, "Play ball!" And with that, game number 7 of the 1960 World Series began.

In the top of the first inning, Vern Law got all three batters he faced to either ground out or pop out. In the top of the first, the Pirates sent five batters to the plate, including Bob Skinner and first baseman Rocky Nelson. With two out, Skinner walked, and Nelson hit a 380-foot home run to right field. Clemente popped out to second base to end the innings. So to the delight of their fans, the Pirates took an early 2–0 lead after one inning.

The Yankees again failed to score in the top of the second. After Pirates catcher Smokey Burgess singled to lead off the bottom of the second, the Yankees made a pitching change and brought in Bill Stafford who promptly walked Don Hoak and gave up a single to Bill Mazeroski. So with the bases loaded and no one out, pitcher Vern Law came to the plate and hit into a double play which allowed Hoak to move to third base and Mazeroski to second. Now with two outs in the inning, center fielder Bill Verdon came to bat and hit a single to right field, driving into score both Hoak and Mazeroski. Dick Groat hit a weak grounder to third to end the inning. The Pirate fans were now going nuts. After only two innings, the Pirates were leading 4–0 over the mighty Yankees.

Their hopes were short-lived, however, as the Yankees' Bill Skowron hit a solo home run in the top of the fifth innings (one of twelve hits he had in this World Series). The Yankees would then score four more runs in the top of the sixth inning, highlighted by a three-run home run by Yankee left fielder, Yogi Berra. During that inning, the Pirates removed starting pitcher Vern Law and replaced him with Elroy Face who was responsible for surrendering all of the Yankees' four runs. The Pirates failed to score in their half of the inning, so after six innings, the Yankees now took the lead, 5–4, over the Pirates.

After the Yankees failed to score in the top of the seventh inning, everyone in the ballpark, including the Pryzinski foursome, stood for the seventh-inning stretch. Ironically, the seventh inning stretch became a baseball tradition that began back in 1910 in Pittsburgh when President William Howard Taft, on a visit to Pittsburgh, went to a baseball game and stood up to stretch in the seventh inning. The crowd, thinking the chief executive was about to leave, stood up out of respect for the office. As Peter Pryzinski arose from his seat to participate in the stretch, he suddenly felt lightheaded and collapsed back into to his seat. Few noticed until after everyone sat down, but it was clear that Peter was in distress. Fortunately for him, the ushers who were so attentive to them when they got to the game noticed that Peter was having problems and came to his aid.

By that time, everyone sitting around their foursome also became aware of the situation and also offered their help. "Let's get him to the infirmary quick!" said one of the ushers.

The Pirates had a small office located at the front entrance of the ballpark that they had converted to an infirmary earlier in the regular season due in part to the large number of fans who attended the Pirates games that year. The infirmary was staffed by two nurses along with several EMTs who were available to transport anyone to nearby Mercy Hospital, if needed. As Peter was brought into the infirmary, the nurses instructed him to lie down on a bed, where they took his blood pressure and checked his heart rate. By this time, Peter was barely conscious but could hear the attending nurse when she said, "This man is having a heart attack! We need to get him to the hospital, STAT!"

Young Daniel stood next to his father and didn't know what to say. He, Ben, and Adam had followed Peter from his seat to the infirmary and were now crowded into the small room together. "Please, God, don't let my daddy die," Daniel prayed as the EMTs placed Peter on a gurney and loaded him onto the waiting ambulance. Daniel could see the EMTs feverishly working on his father as they closed the ambulance doors.

"You guys can ride up front with me," the ambulance driver instructed. Everything was happening so fast for Daniel, and as he stepped into the front of the ambulance, all he could think of was his father. Baseball, the Pirates, and the World Series were no longer of any importance to him. His father was too young to die. He didn't want to lose him and continued his prayers. "God, please don't let him die. I love him so much."

As the ambulance pulled away from Forbes Field, sirens blaring, no one inside could hear the cheering that was erupting behind them from the fans who were attending game number 7 of the 1960 World Series.

Chapter 31

World Champions

The last two innings of the 1960 World Series involved some of the most unusual, unexpected, and dramatic plays in the history of Major League Baseball. These plays, including those that took place during the first seven innings of this game, have made the seventh game of the 1960 World Series the greatest baseball game ever played, at least for twists and turns in the opinion of many.

The seventh inning of this game ended with neither team scoring a run. Although there were no runs scored, one of the most significant events in this game, and in the history of baseball, took place that few baseball historians ever make note of. It involved the substitution of a player by the Pittsburgh Pirates.

Smoky Burgess was the starting catcher for the Pirates. During the 1960 regular season, Smoky played in 110 games and was at bat 337 times and hit for an average of .294. He collected 99 hits, scored 33 runs, and hit 7 home runs. He also drove in 33 runs. He was a dependable and durable catcher. "Standing in at a pudgy five-eight," Burgess was saddled with such unflattering descriptions as "a walking laundry bag" and "barely fit enough to play for the Moose Lodge softball team."

"Physical conditioning aside, nobody debated that Smoky Burgess could hit at any time, against any pitcher, in any situation," proclaimed Andy Sturgill in his book, *Sweet '60: The 1960 Pittsburgh Pirates* (SABR, 2 April 2013, p. 16).

Needless to say, Smoky was also not the fastest base runner in the Pirates' ball club, so when Smoky singled into center field to lead off the top on seventh inning for the Pirates, manager Danny Murtaugh quickly brought into the game the speedy Joe Christopher to pinch run for Burgess. Backup catcher Hal Smith would replace Burgess in the lineup and would be batting sixth.

At the end of seven innings, the Yankees held a slim 5–4 over the Pirates. That would soon change as the Yankees scored two more runs in the top of the eighth highlighted by a walk to Yogi Berra, singles by Bill Skowron, Johnny Blanchard, and a double by Clete Boyer all off of reliefer Elroy Face. So at the end of seven and a half innings, the Yankees widened their lead to 7–4.

If you ask any average baseball fan and some experts, many would likely deny that they ever heard of a little-known baseball player by the name of Hal Smith. Ironically, Smith had signed with the New York Yankees in 1949 but never played with the Yankees. He joined the Pirates at the beginning of the 1960 season after playing with the Baltimore Orioles and the Kansas City Athletics and played third base and catcher for the Pirates. He saw limited action during the 1960 regular season and only batted .223 but did manage to hit eleven home runs. Even though he would never become a household name, what would follow for Hal Smith in the bottom of the eighth inning was something that would forever change his life and the course of the seventh game of the 1960 World Series.

The bottom of the eighth inning began with Gino Cimoli pinch hitting for Elroy Face and batting ninth and promptly hitting a single to center field off of Yankee reliefer, Bobby Shantz. Bill Virdon followed Cimoli in the lineup and hit what appeared to be a sure double play ball to Yankee shortstop, Tony Kubek. In what is considered one of the craziest plays in World Series history, the ball that was hit to Kubek took a last second crazy hop off the infield ground at Forbes Field and struck Kubek in the throat, rendering him almost unconscious. So instead of there being two outs in the inning, both Pirate runners were safe with no outs. Joe DeMaestri then replaced Tony Kubek at shortstop as Kubek was unable to continue playing.

Dick Groat was the third batter in the inning and hit a single through the hole between shortstop and third base, which scored Cimoli from second and enabled Virdon to move to second in scoring position. Following the hit by Groat, Yankees manager Casey Stengel brought in relief pitcher, Jim Coates. The move appeared to be a good one as Coates got Bob Skinner to ground out and Rocky Nelson to fly out. The Yankees needed only one more out to get out of the inning, when the speedy upstart right fielder Roberto Clemente came to the plate. Clemente had been signed by then general manager of the Pirates Branch Rickey and made his major league debut with the Pirates on April 17, 1955. He was also the first Latin American to play in the Major League (it was also Rickey who had signed Jackie Robinson to a Major League contract when he was the general manager of the Brooklyn Dodgers.)

So with two outs and two on, Clemente hit a weak infield grounder which appeared to be a sure out, but as was his style, Clemente was able to outrun the fielders and was called safe at first base in what should have been the inning ending third out. The play enabled Virdon to score to cut the Yankees lead to 7–6. In an inning that should have ended with no runs being scored by the Pirates, the Yankees were now faced with the possibility of the Pirates tying the game or even taking the lead, when Hal Smith came to the plate with two on and two out at the bottom of the eighth inning. What happened next changed the course of this game and would result in the most fantastic ninth inning in the history of the World Series. With the count 2–2, Coates pitched to Smith who then hit a three-run home run over deep left field to give the Pirates a 9–7 lead over the Yankees. After hitting this home run, the Yankees made another pitching change and brought in reliefer Ralph Terry. Don Hoak hit a fly ball to left field to end the inning.

Needless to say, the partisan fans at Forbes Field were going crazy. Their Pirates were only three outs from winning the 1960 World Series. They would soon learn that things would not be that easy as the mighty Yankees refused to give up.

The Pirates brought in Bob Friend to pitch to the Yankees in the top of the ninth, in hopes of protecting the lead and saving the win for the Pirates. It was not to be Bob Friend's game, however, as he quickly gave up singles to Bobby Richardson and Dale Long. So, with two on and no one out, the Pirates made another pitching change bringing in game 5 hero Harvey Haddix. Haddix quickly got the first out, when Roger Maris popped out behind home plate. He was not so lucky with the next batter, Mickey Mantle, who hit a single to right field, which scored Richardson from second base.

The margin of victory for the Pirates had been cut to one run with only one out. Gil McDougald was called in to pinch run for Dale Long at third base while Mickey Mantle remained at first when Yogi Berra came to the plate. In what is considered another one of the craziest plays in World Series history, Yogi Berra hit a sharp ground ball to Pirates first baseman, Rocky Nelson, in what appears to be a sure double play that would end the inning and the game. Nelson grabbed the grounder, stepped on first base for the second out. For some reason, Mantle did not break for second base but decided to go back to first and slide back safe under the tag of Nelson. This play enabled McDougald to score the tying run from third. Bill Skowron then grounded into a force-out at second to end the inning. Unfortunately for the Pirates, the damage was done. They had let the Yankees back into the game, thanks in part to one of the most unusual plays in World Series history.

With both Whitey Ford and Ralph Terry warming up in the bullpen, manager Casey Stengel elected to have Terry pitch to the Pirates at the bottom of the eighth inning. Instead of bringing in Whitey Ford to pitch to the Pirates in the bottom of the ninth, Stengel elected to stay with Terry, a mistake that would eventually cost Stengel his job.

Ralph Terry was a right-hand pitcher who opened his baseball career with the New York Yankees. During the 1960 regular season, Terry had posted a win loss record of 10–8 with an ERA of 3.40. Pitching the top of the ninth inning marked his second appearance in the 1960 World Series. He would be pitching to the Pirates second baseman Bill Mazeroski, who was the eighth batter in the Pirates lineup for game 7.

Bill had collected one hit earlier in the game but had made no other significant impact on the scoring by the Pirates. Johnny Blanchard was the Yankees catcher who had started the game behind the plate. He was the third-string catcher behind Yogi Berra and Elston Howard. The Yankees scouting report on Mazeroski was that he liked the ball up. What he didn't want was a fastball down at the knees. On his first pitch to Mazeroski, Terry threw a high-breaking ball outside without much on it, which Maz took for a ball. Blanchard immediately called time-out and began walking to the mound to tell Terry that he should be throwing fastballs down.

Blanchard would later recall that Terry told him that in no uncertain terms to get back behind the plate and that he was going to throw the pitches he wanted. On the second pitch to Mazeroski, Terry threw him another high breaking ball which Maz hit over the 406-foot marker in left-center field in Forbes Field to end the game, making the 1960 Pittsburgh Pirates the World Champions of baseball. Following his home run, Maz made one of the most-famous trips around the bases in baseball history, and the fans in Forbes Field and in Pittsburgh Pennsylvania went crazy. To this day, Mazeroski's home run has been the only walk off home run hit in the seventh and deciding game of a World Series.

During an interview following the game, Hal Smith would comment on national TV that "the Yankees broke all the records, but that the Pirates were World Champions." The Yankees had been the heavy favorites against the Pirates, the upstart winners of the National League. The Yankees scored 55 runs, the most runs scored by any one team in World Series history, and more than twice as many as the Pirates, who scored 27. Pittsburgh had won three games: 6–4, 3–2, and 5–2. The Yankees had won three games: 16–3, 10–0, and 12–0 (game 6 in Pittsburgh). Then came game 7 on October 13, 1960, with its many twists and turns. In this game, there were 19 runs, 24 hits in a game that was played in 2 hours, 36 minutes. There was also not a single strikeout recorded by the nine pitchers used (Yankees 5, Pirates 4).

*****

In nearby Mercy Catholic hospital, Daniel Pryzinski stood in front of a statue of St. Joseph where he had stood praying ever since his father was admitted in critical condition. Unbeknownst to Daniel at the time, his father had suffered a massive heart attack, which would require him to undergo open-heart surgery. "Please don't let him die, St. Joseph. I'll do anything you ask, but don't let him die." He was standing in front of the statue when his mother and brothers arrived at the hospital.

Along with Ben and Adam Brodziak, the group joined together in the waiting room located outside of the area where Peter Pryzinski was having his surgery. After arriving at the hospital, Pauline Pryzinski was able to advise the attending physician about the chest pains her husband had been experiencing over the past several weeks. This information was important to determine the course of action the hospital needed to take to treat Peter. They had been in the hospital for around two hours before Pauline was advised that the surgeons were going to have to perform emergency open-heart surgery.

The rest of the group did not take this announcement well, and it was Ben Brodziak who had recommended that they go to the hospital's chapel to pray for Peter's safe recovery. It was agreed that Pauline would stay behind to wait for any word from the doctors as the rest made their way to the chapel. As Ben left the waiting room, he noticed a calendar hanging behind the attending nurse's station. The calendar reminded him that the date was October 13, 1960, which was Feast Day of the last of the visions by Our Blessed Virgin Mary at Fatima back on October 13, 1917. How ironic, he thought, that the seventh game of the 1960 World Series would also be played on this date. After leaving Forbes Field, Ben had lost all track of time. He now wondered which team won the game.

Ben Brodziak always carried his Rosaries with him no matter where he went, so it was he who led the rest in prayer. "God, we are here to pray for the quick recovery of our friend Peter Pryzinski. Please watch over him and help guide his surgeons in the performance of their duties. In the name of the Father, the Son, and the Holy Ghost." Even though no one else had a Rosary with them, they all knew how to pray it and followed as Ben prayed all five decades.

Daniel had been silent during the recitation of the Rosary, preferring to pray in silence to St. Joseph. It was to St. Joseph that Daniel had often prayed during the many days and nights he had endured when his father had come home drunk.

Subconsciously, St. Joseph had become a second father to him, one he could rely upon to talk to in absence of his real father. Before he had started to drink, his father was a strong and devoted father, just like St. Joseph. Now that his father was recovering from his alcoholism, he was becoming more like the father he once knew and one that he desperately needed back in his life. He didn't want to lose him now after all his father had gone through to make him well. So Daniel decided to stay in the chapel to continue his prayers long after the others left to return to the waiting room.

*****

It was a little past midnight when he was awakened in the pew where he had fallen asleep. "Daniel, your father's out of surgery and is doing well." It was Ben Brodziak who had been keeping an eye out for Daniel during the long night. "Wake up, son. Your mom wants us all together."

Daniel rubbed his eyes, trying to regain his composure. "Is everything okay? How is my dad?" Daniel inquired.

"He's doing fine. He had a tough time of it, but he's going to make it through."

Daniel jumped up and followed Ben back into the waiting room. His mother was standing with the rest of the family, crying and smiling at the same time. She grabbed Daniel as soon as she saw him and gave him a big hug. "Your dad is doing fine. He's sleeping right now. I'm the only one that the doctors will allow in his room, but he's making a good recovery. You'll probably be able to see him later on in the day once he is awake. But everything is fine, thank God. Oh, by the way, I also want you to know that the Pirates beat the Yankees. They are World Champions. Do you believe it?"

Daniel had completely forgotten about the game. Ever since leaving the game in the ambulance, Daniel could not think of anything else but his father. It was the bottom of the eighth inning by the time the ambulance left Forbes Field on its way to Mercy Hospital. The roar that they never heard from inside the ambulance were the fans celebrating Hal Smith's three-run home run. It wasn't until the next day that he learned about the ninth inning and Bill Mazeroski's walk-off home run.

It had been a magical year in more ways than one, not only for the Pittsburgh Pirates but also for the Pryzinski family. His beloved Pittsburgh Pirates were the champions of the world, and his hero, Bill Mazeroski, had won the game with his walk-off home run. Through the grace of God and with the help of family and friends, his father was on the road to becoming free from his alcohol addiction, and he was also recovering from a near fatal heart attack. Most important of all, during the year 1960, Daniel Pryzinski met and made friends with Adam Brodziak. The boys would forever remember the times that shared together in 1960 and how their love of God, family, and baseball enabled them to overcome hardships and experience joys, which would help to strengthen the friendship that would last their lifetimes.

Chapter 32

Number 406

City of Champions

Angel number 406 symbolizes abundance and prosperity. It's a sign from the universe that the hard work you've been putting in will pay off, and you will soon reap the rewards. This number is also a symbol of balance and harmony. To the City of Pittsburgh and the people living there, this number will always be remembered for Bill Mazeroski's famous home run in the 1960 World Series. The 406 section of the wall over which he hit his famous home run in Forbes Field was preserved following the demolition of the ball park on July 28, 1971. The 1960 Pittsburgh Pirates were a bunch of hardworking blue-collar type of guys, who never gave up, helping them to achieve a dream come true, winning the 1960 World Series baseball championship. It also marked the beginning of a renaissance in professional sports in the City of Pittsburgh that would eventually earn the city the nickname of "the City of Champions."

The three professional sports teams in Pittsburgh—the Steelers, the Penguins, and the Pirates—would combine to go on to win sixteen World Championships. The Pirates would win the title again in 1970 and in 1979. The Steelers would win six Super Bowls, including four from 1975 to 1979, and the Pittsburgh Penguins would win five Stanley Cups. Even the short-lived Pittsburgh Condors captured an ABA basketball championship led by Connie Hawkins in 1967.

Not to be outdone, the Pittsburgh Panthers captured one of their nine NCAA National Football Championships in 1976.

At the same time, a young upcoming golf pro from nearby Latrobe, Pennsylvania (forty miles from downtown Pittsburgh), by the name of Arnold Palmer was coming onto the scene. In 1960, Palmer won the Master Tournament and the US Open. He was named PGA Player of the Year in 1960 and 1961. He developed a close relationship with the steelworkers from Pittsburgh, who went out of their way to see Palmer play, no matter where. These devoted fans were later to be nicknamed "Arnie's Army." His popularity gave rise to a new brand of golfing enthusiasts.

Golf no longer was the sport of the rich and privileged. Blue-collar workers from Pittsburgh and around the country began taking to the sport. This resulted in an explosion in the sale of golf equipment along with the construction of many new golf courses needed to accommodate the increase in the demand to play golf. The game would never be the same thanks to Arnold Palmer.

The Pittsburgh area would also go on to produce six of the twenty-three quarterbacks currently in the NFL Hall of Fame. These quarterbacks include George Blanda (Youngwood, Pennsylvania), Johnny Unitas (Pittsburgh, Pennsylvania), Joe Namath (Beaver Falls, Pennsylvania), Joe Montana (New Eagle, Pennsylvania), Dan Marino (Pittsburgh, Pennsylvania), and Jim Kelly (Pittsburgh/East Brady, Pennsylvania).

While all of this success was happening, Pittsburgh itself was forced to undergo a complete metamorphization. In 1979, the steel industry in America underwent a complete collapse due in part to two recessions very close together: one from 1973–1975 and one in 1980. This collapse forced the steel industry to lay off thousands of steel workers. The hardest hit were those working in Pittsburgh. Many of these workers were forced to relocate from Pittsburgh to other parts of the county in order to find work. The one constant that continues to draw them together, no matter where they moved, has been their beloved and highly successful sports teams, the most prominent of which were the Pittsburgh Steelers.

Although the professional sports teams in Pittsburgh have won sixteen championships, ironically, only the 1960 Pittsburgh Pirates World Series win was played at home. The rest were won on the road. Pittsburgh is also the only city in America where all of their sports teams wear the same colors, black and gold.

Call it luck, hard work, talent, or sports karma or a combination of all, these are some of the reasons Pittsburgh teams have enjoyed such success since Bill Mazeroski hit his walk-off home run in 1960. Over the years since then, Pittsburgh sports teams have produced such legendary players as Roberto Clemente, Willie Stargell, Terry Bradshaw, Lynn Swan, Mean Joe Green, Franco Harris, Mario Lemieux, Sydney Crosby, Jaromír Jágr, Evgeni Malkin, and of course, Bill Mazeroski. In addition to all of these legendary talents sports, karma has also come into play. The Pittsburgh Pirates were the first to draft and start a Latino player in Roberto Clemente. In September of 1970, the Pirates were the first Major League Baseball team to field an all African American/Latino starting lineup. The Rooney family, the long time, and original owners of the Pittsburgh Steelers are devout Catholics who are the only team in the NFL who doesn't have cheerleaders. The Rooneys feel that such a practice degrades women.

From 1969 to the present, the Steelers have only had three head coaches, all of whom are in the hall of fame or who will be eventually elected to the hall of fame. After winning two Stanley Cups, Mario Lemieux retired and assumed ownership of the franchise in 1999, following the near collapse of the team in Pittsburgh. Mario went on to draft several key players including Sydney Crosby and has gone on to three more Stanley cups as the team's owner. But the most significant of all was Mazeroski's home run, which started it all.

The City of Pittsburgh has survived the loss of the steel industry and has been able to transform itself from a dirty, smokey, polluted city to one of the cleanest and most beautiful in the country. The city was able to leverage its technology and higher education and financial services to successfully move on from its steelmaking past history. Pittsburgh's annual unemployment rate continuously outperforms the rest of the nation and its strong family-based and faith-driven, almost Midwest like mentality makes it a friendly and safe place to live and work and visit. PNC Park, the current home of the Pittsburgh Pirates, is considered one of the most beautiful baseball parks in all of Major League Baseball.

All of this started with one home run that was hit in the greatest baseball game ever played. When you watch the replay of this home run, the last thing one sees is Yogi Berra looking up as the baseball sails over the 406 sign in left field. "Kiss it goodbye," Pirate announcer Bob Prince would say. The rest is history.

Epilogue

In the play *The Bronx Tale*, the opening scene takes place in the Bronx, New York, in 1960. The main character, Young Calogero, refers to the 1960 World Series and says, "Bill Mazeroski, I hate him. He made Mickey Mantle cry. The papers said the Mick cried." So it went for many of the Yankee fans following the 1960 World Series. It had been a devastating loss.

The Pirates fans, on the other hand, were elated, including Daniel Pryzinski and his friend, Adam Brodziak. The Brodziaks would stay with the Pryzinskis for another week following the release of Peter Pryzinski from the Mercy Hospital after having his open-heart surgery. Peter had suffered what doctors refer to as a widow-maker. A widow-maker is an informal term for a heart attack that involves 100 percent blockage in the left anterior descending (LAD) artery. In 1960, almost all such heart attacks were fatal.

Peter was lucky and fortunate that his heart attack had occurred at Forbes Field, where he was seen almost immediately at the infirmary. If he had been at home, he likely would not have made it to the hospital in time. Although he would eventually fully recover, Peter's heart was so badly damaged that he would not be able to ever return to work as a steelworker. He applied for and received full permanent disability benefits from the union. The money he received from these disability benefits provided enough income for Peter to support his family.

Peter also continued to recover from his alcoholism and remained sober for the rest of his life, never again touching a drop of drink. He became a stay-at-home dad and became involved in every aspect of his family's life. He cooked dinner every night for his family, did all the grocery shopping, and continued to be a loving husband to his wife. He volunteered as a mentor for his local alcoholics anonymous group and was able to help many men and women to overcome their addition to alcohol. He would also attend daily Mass at Immaculate Heart of Mary Church and never forgot to thank God for all that he was given. He lived to be eighty-five years old.

With her husband staying at home and attending to the family, Pauline Pryzinski decided to return to school where she eventually earned her BS in nursing. After graduating, she started to work in the operating room at Mercy Hospital where her husband had his surgery. She retired from Mercy as the chief operating nurse of the staff. She died a year after her husband. The two would go on to have ten grandchildren and two great-grandchildren.

Bill Mazeroski would finish his baseball career with the Pirates where he retired and played his last game on October 4, 1972, for the Pittsburgh Pirates. He left the game, earning a career-batting average of .260 with 2016 hits, 138 home runs, and 853 runs batted in. He was inducted into the baseball Hall of Fame in 2001. He is still alive and resides in Panama City, Florida.

Hal Smith remained with the Pirates for one more year, following the 1960 season before he was traded to the Houston Colts. He played his last game in the Major League on July 22, 1964, while playing for the Cincinnati Reds. He achieved a lifetime batting average of .267, hit 58 home runs, and had 323 runs batted in. He died on January 9, 2020, at the age of eighty-nine.

Daniel Pryzinski would attend Notre Dame college after graduating from High School. He would later go to John Hopkins medical school where he studied to be a cardiologist. After graduating from medical school, Daniel returned to Pittsburgh, where he became a prominent cardiovascular surgeon. He would also volunteer his time treating men and women at the local Alcohol and Drug Rehabilitation Center in Pittsburgh. He would never forget what the Somerset Rehabilitation Center had done for his father to help overcome his alcoholism.

Adam Brodziak would realize his lifelong dream of becoming a racehorse veterinarian. After graduating from veterinarian school, he would relocate to Kentucky where he would become a well-known and trusted vet for all of the major thoroughbred racehorse farms. The highlight of his career was being hired by Claiborne Farm to be the veterinarian for the great racehorse Secretariat after the horse retired from racing in 1973. He cared for the horse until his death in 1989. After retiring, Daniel returned to Windber and purchased the old Thiele farm, where he and his family would live and raise thoroughbred racehorses.

Adam and Peter would remain close friends for the rest of their lives. They would trade off visiting one another at least once a year. They attended both the 1971 and 1979 World Series, both of which were won by the Pittsburgh Pirates.

Ben and Kathryn Brodziak lived in their home in Windber well into their nineties. They died one month apart. They, too, remained close friends with the Pryzinski family. Pauline and Peter were forever grateful for all the help they had given them in the summer of 1960. Shortly after retiring from the coal mines, Ben developed coal miner's black lung disease, but was able to lead an overwise healthy life. Both remained active in their Parish and in the community of Windber. They also spent many hours volunteering at the Somerset County Alcohol and Drug Rehabilitation Center.

Dr. Tom Slevic eventually gave up his private practice and took over as the full-time Director of the Somerset County Alcohol and Drug Rehabilitation Center. He pioneered the treatment and counseling of retired military veterans and worked closely with the Veterans Administration in the care of servicemen suffering from post-traumatic stress disorder (PTSD). He would eventually help veterans who had served in World War II, the Korean War, Vietnam, and Gulf Wars. After his death, the Somerset County Alcohol and Drug Rehabilitation Center was renamed the Tom Slevic Center in his honor.

Ralph Terry would go on to pitch with the New York Yankees unit 1964 when he was traded to the Cleveland Indians. Following the 1960 loss to the Pittsburgh Pirates, the Yankees would go on to win the 1961 and 1962 World Series. In the 1962 regular season, Terry went 23–12 with a 3.19 ERA and led the AL in wins. He would later be named the MVP of the 1962 World Series. He retired from baseball in 1967 after posting a career win loss record of 107–99. He died in 2022 at the age of eighty-six.

Roberto Clemente would become the greatest of all to play for the Pittsburgh Pirates. He played his entire career from 1955 to 1972 with the Pirates. During that time, he participated in fifteen All-Star games, won NL batting titles in 1961, 1964, 1965, 1967, and was named the NL MVP in 1966. He was also named MVP of the 1971 World Series. His life came to a tragic end on December 31, 1972, when the plane he was flying in carrying relief supplies to earthquake ridden Nicaragua crashed after taking off from Puerto Rico. His body was never recovered.

In 1960, the Pittsburgh Pirates were owned in part by actor signer Bing Crosby. The seventh game of the 1960 World Series had been nationally televised by NBC. The Pirates regular season announcer, Bob Prince announced the first half of the seventh game of the World Series while the Yankees announcer, Mel Allen, announced the second half of the game. Prince was on his way to the Pirates locker room to interview players after the game and never saw Mazeroski's epic home run. Years later, the NBC tapes of game 7 were found in the wine cellar of Bing Crosby's home after he died. ESPN purchased the tapes and converted them to DVD where they were sold to the public as part of the fiftieth anniversary of game 7.

In 2010, ESPN celebrated the fiftieth anniversary by broadcasting a televised replay of the game hosted by Bob Costas. The event was attended by many of the Pirates who played in that game, including Hal Smith, Dick Groat, Vernon Law, Bill Virdon. Pittsburgh Steelers legend Franko Harris, and native-born Pittsburgh actor Michael Keaton was also in attendance.

Bibliography

————. "A History of Polish Hill and the PHCA." *Wikipedia.* Retrieved December 22, 2006.

Barbey, Daniel E., vice admiral USN (ret.). *MacArthur's Amphibious Navy: Seventh Amphibious Force Operations 1943–1945.*

Baseball reference. https://www.baseball-reference.com.

Baseball's Greatest Games: 1960 World Series Game 7, DVD by ESPN.

Calvocoressi, Peter, Guy Wint, John Pritchard. *The Penguin History of the Second World War.* London: Penguin, 1999.

Clemente, Roberto. *Wikipedia.* www.https://en.wikipedia.org/wiki/ Roberto_Clemente.

Demolition of Forbes Field Historic Pittsburgh. www.https://historicpittsburgh.org/islandora/object/pitt%3AFORF06UA.

Forbes Field. *Wikipedia.* www.https://en.wikipedia.org/wiki/Forbes_ Field.

Hixson, Walter L. *The American Experience in World War II: The United States and the Road to War in Europe.* Taylor & Francis, 2003. ISBN 978-0-415-94029-0. Archived from the original on 2015-09-06. Retrieved 2016-06-04.

June 6, 2015. https://www.steelers.com/news/western-pa-home-to-hall-of-fame-qbs-15377429#:~:text=%2D%20George%20 Blanda%20(Youngwood%2C%20Pa,East%20Brady%2C%20 Pa.

Morris, Zach S. *When the Beaches Trembled.*

Pittsburgh Steelers website, Western Pennsylvania, home to Hall of Fame QBs.

Prefer, Nathan N. *Leyte, 1944: The Soldiers' Battle*. Havertown, PA: Casemate Publishers, 2012.

Sandomir, Richard. *The New York Times, 50 Years Later, a Slide Still Confounds*. September 30, 2010.

Star Tribune. https://www.startribune.com/bill-mazeroski-home-run-1960-world-series-johnny-blanchard-minneapolis-catcher-pirates-yankees.

The National Shrine of Our Lady of Czestochowa website. www. https://czestochowa.us.

This Day in History. "Draft Age Is Lowered to 18." https://www.history.com/this-day-in-history/draft-age-is-lowered-to-18.

Visit Pittsburgh. https://www.visitpittsburgh.com/media/g20-pittsburgh-summit/transformation-city.

About the Author

Joseph J. Badowski grew up in the small coal-mining town of Windber, Pennsylvania, which is nestled high up in the Allegheny Mountains of Western Pennsylvania. His father, both his grandfathers, all his uncles, and one of his three brothers were all coal miners. From his father and mother, he learned the value of hard work, the importance of a strong family, the need for a good education, and most importantly, the value of being a good Catholic.

After attending his first eight years of school in a Catholic school, he went on to graduate from Windber Area High School. He then attended Temple University in Philadelphia, where he graduated from in 1976 with a degree in business administration. After graduating from college, he got a job with Liberty Mutual Insurance Company and would spend the rest of his forty-five-year career in the insurance industry. He retired in 2021 after spending the last nineteen years of his career working for Nationwide Insurance Company.

He met his wife, Kathy O'Donnell, in 1975, and they got married in 1978. They have one son, Matthew, who is married to his beautiful wife, Melissa Siminski Badowski. They have three wonderful children—Emma, Harper, and Carter. They live in Mount Laurel, New Jersey, and belong to Our Lady of Good Counsel Parish in Moorestown, New Jersey. He is a member of Council 1082 of the Knights of Columbus and serves as a eucharist minister for the parish.

He is an avid cyclist, fisherman, skier, golfer, and he loves the outdoors.

Printed in the USA
CPSIA information can be obtained
at www.ICGtesting.com
CBHW030730260824
13628CB00010B/268